Couples Guide

To

Emotional
Intelligence

*EQ Mastery For Better Conflict
Resolution, Perfect
Communication, And Increased
Intimacy To Improve Your
Relationship*

JAMIE BRYCE

CONTENTS

INTRODUCTION

JAMIE BRYCE

Thank you for purchasing *Couples Guide To Emotional Intelligence*, and congratulations on having the initiative to take control and make improvements in your life and relationship. Here's a brief overview of what you can expect from this book:

This book starts by defining what the psychological concept of emotional intelligence is, including its scientific and research histories, to provide context and a deeper understanding of its impact and value. Then we will move to the specific ways a higher emotional intelligence can improve a relationship. Next, it will discuss how you can build your emotional intelligence up, and put what you build into practice.

The next four chapters focus on the four key parts of emotional intelligence—self-awareness, self-regulation, social awareness, and social regulation. At this point, we'll discuss what roles each of these components specifically plays in your relationship, and we'll also provide tools and strategies to help you improve your abilities in these areas—strategies that can also be applied to your dealings with your partner.

The last chapter gives you a chance to practice how to use your newfound understanding of emotional intelligence and its four key parts to solve relationship issues with several hypothetical exercises.

Having a higher emotional intelligence really can help you build better, lasting relationships, and the strategies in this book can help get you there!

NOTE: Emotional intelligence (EI for short) is also referred to by many other names that can be interchangeably used to describe the concept. These other names include emotional quotient (EQ for short), emotional literacy, and many others that you may come across in conversation about emotional intelligence.

CHAPTER 1:

WHY RELATIONSHIPS FAIL, AND WHY HIGH EMOTIONAL INTELLIGENCE OFFERS THE SOLUTION

JAMIE BRYCE

Why do relationships fail? What makes a strong marriage of 20-plus years collapse into divorce*? Why do so many romantic relationships break up a little after the two-year point? How does something that starts off so right, so perfect, end up falling apart?

It certainly isn't for lack of trying. People have been looking for solutions for failing relationships since the beginning of the written word (and probably even before). Everything from the Bible to Buzzfeed has a theory on why most relationships fail, and probably ten times as many theories on how to save them.

Failing relationships is an old problem. Maybe one of the oldest. It's also a problem that people are still grappling with today, hence the near-endless amount of self-help articles that appear when you Google "How can I save my relationship?"

If you've opened this book, chances are you're searching for an answer to the same question. Chances are you've already searched through Google and read all the *7 Tips For This*, *5 Ways To Do That* articles.

Chances are you've already tried the advice from those articles that sounded like it would be a good answer to your relationship problems (*Spend more time together, Schedule a date night...*), and maybe even some of the advice that deep down you knew was no good, but was maybe still worth a try (*Play hard to get, Be mysterious...*) Chances are, you're finally ready for some real answers.

* Divorced? You're Not Alone!

There can be a lot of feelings of stress and social stigma around divorce, and some of those feelings are completely justified. After all, you're splitting up properties, changing living arrangements, possibly even negotiating visitation rights for children. Any of those things would be incredibly stressful, and trying to manage all three can be a lot for anyone.

What shouldn't stress you about divorce though, is how frequently it happens. If you're feeling like a social pariah because you got divorced—don't. About 45 percent of marriages end in divorce, so you're far from alone in splitting up. While unfortunate, statistically speaking, divorce is a common component of modern life.

Conversely, if you're worried that your marriage will

end in divorce because the statistics are so high, don't be. It can seem logical to think, "Well, since about 45 percent of marriages end in divorce, my marriage has barely more than a 50 percent chance of lasting," but this reasoning is a bit backward.

Think of divorce statistics as a descriptive tool, rather than a predictive tool. The current data on divorces is presented as statistics to describe what divorces look like in the world as it is at the moment. Divorce statistics do not predict or otherwise control how many divorces must be happening at a given point in time.

What does this mean for you? It means the divorce statistics don't define you, you define the divorce statistics. They have no control over you, you're the one who has control over them, just like you have control over your life and marriage.

Whether your marriage succeeds or fails, it's because of the choices you and your partner make, and not because of any statistical averages, no matter how negative they may seem.

It's also important to remember that these divorce statistics are incredibly broad, lumping every single sociological group into one big, broad statistic. Inside that big statistic, there's actually a ton of variety among different sociological populations. For example, *Pew Research* reports that college-educated women married between 2006 and 2010 have a 78 percent chance of their marriage lasting at least 20 years.

There is a multitude of other factors that can affect a group's divorce rate besides age, sex, and education level. Religion, career, location, really every social detail you can think of can affect the divorce rate of a social group one way or the other.

So, because your personal sociological details can greatly affect your average likelihood of divorce, it doesn't make much sense to worry about the average national divorce rate, since it's very likely it doesn't apply to your personal social group.

Emotional Intelligence, And Why It's The Key To A Successful Relationship

The problem with so much relationship advice out there (we're looking at you, Buzzfeed), and the many things we do to try and fix our relationships, is that it addresses symptoms of a struggling relationship, but not the core problems that are actually causing those symptoms.

Think of it this way: When you take Tylenol for a headache, you're not actually curing the headache. You're taking a temporary painkiller that alleviates the bad feelings you're having for a while. Sometimes, the Tylenol numbs the pain long enough for a headache to pass on its own, so we say that it "works" as a medical solution to headaches. But, we'd never call Tylenol a "cure" for headaches, because we know it's not.

We've all experienced headaches that come back after Tylenol wears off, and we've all experienced pains that Tylenol doesn't relieve. And we're okay with that because that's what we expect from Tylenol. We know it's not something that cures headaches, it's something that makes the pain symptoms go away while a headache cures itself.

The problem is that a lot of us are treating our relationships like we treat our headaches—meaning we're applying temporary solutions to pain symptoms, rather than addressing the root causes of the pain.

A suffering relationship is not like a headache. You can't just apply a common quick fix that might take some of the pain away for a while, then hope what's really wrong will just work itself out in the meantime. But, so much of the relationship advice out there, and so much of what we do to try and fix our own relationships is just that: a quick, painkilling fix that does not address what's actually wrong. This is why so much of it fails.

Like trying to fix a headache, people tend to approach fixing their relationship problems in a top-down, solution-first way.

"We're fighting too much. I think we should talk more."

"I don't trust him/her. I'll just take a quick peek at their phone to see who they're texting to ease my peace my mind."

"I don't want to see my in-laws this weekend. I'll just tell a white lie about work to get out of it."

While any of these "solutions" might work short-term, they don't address the core reasons for the problems. Is not talking enough really why you're fighting all the time? Is the reason you don't trust your partner because you can't see what's happening on their phone? Is lying to get out of one visit with your in-laws really the solution you want?

To really solve any of these relationship problems, you need to address the cause of the problem and not the symptoms. Why are you fighting? Why don't you trust your partner? Why do you dread seeing your in-laws?

To answer those questions, and to find real, effective ways to improve your relationships, you need to understand emotional intelligence.

What Is Emotional Intelligence, And Why Is It Key For Helping Relationships Succeed?

"Happy Tears Vs. Sad Tears"

Emotional intelligence is how we describe a person's ability to see, define, and understand the emotions of themselves and others, and also how well they're able to take that emotional information and use it to guide their actions.

It's similar to other measures of intelligence that you may be familiar with, such as IQ (which is used to measure and describe intellectual abilities like memory and logic) or physical intelligence (which measures how much control, skill, and ability a person has with their body). Similarly, emotional intelligence is used as a kind of catch-all term to describe a person's mental abilities along a specific part of intelligence—in this case, emotions. Also, like those other measurements, emotional intelligence has a long history of psychological research and scientific backing (which will be explored in more depth in future chapters.)

Here's a simple example of emotional intelligence in use: You see a person crying. To judge why they're crying, you use your emotional intelligence.

- You see their crying is quiet and soft. They're sniffling, but not really sobbing.

- Their eyes are mostly open. They're standing, sort of hugging themselves.

- In between the quivering of their lips, you can see the person is smiling a bit. They're shaking their head in what looks like disbelief.

Judging by those three points, your emotional intelligence tells you that the person is likely crying out of happiness. You decide to approach the person and ask if they're okay because your emotional intelligence tells you that even though someone is crying out of happiness, they still might need consolation or help because they've become overwhelmed by their emotions.

So, we can see how emotional intelligence was used to help us interpret emotions (why this person is crying) and guide our behavior (determining that this person might need my help to calm down). But, like IQ, emotional intelligence is a term used to describe a range of abilities—and not everyone has the same range. Let's revisit our crying person example with someone who has much lower emotional intelligence.

Someone else sees our happy crying person. Instead of correctly interpreting why they're crying, our person with lower emotional intelligence assumes that they're sad. Because the crying is soft and small, the person decides to try and cheer them up with a joke. They yell, "Hey, who died?!" across the room. This confuses our crying person, who takes the joke to mean that no one wants to see them cry, so they get embarrassed and leave.

Mistaking happy tears for sad ones can be a small and simple mistake to make, but as we can see in the example above, can make a big difference in how an interpersonal interaction plays out.

This is why emotional intelligence is so important and essential for the foundation of successful relationships. Emotional intelligence is what allows us to correctly interpret the emotions not only of our partners but of ourselves as well. It's also what lets us use that emotional information to move past the symptoms of our relationship problems and address the real causes.

Emotional intelligence is important to the health, growth, and success of relationships because it offers a way to affect real change in them. By improving how you interpret and act on emotions, you'll be able to make real, lasting improvements in your current or future relationships. Here are just some of the areas emotional intelligence can help you improve your relationships:

- **Resolve Conflict Better:** Higher emotional intelligence will help you identify conflicts sooner and resolve them faster before they escalate into serious arguments. When serious arguments do happen, you'll be able to diffuse them better and steer the argument toward a more productive and positive conclusion.

- **Learn From Mistakes:** Not only will you learn how to better identify and understand the roots of your mistakes, you also learn to better see how your mistakes affect your partner, making it much easier for you to gain the understanding and motivation to avoid such mistakes in the future.

- **Managing Your Emotions:** High emotional intelligence will help you take control of your emotions, by improving your ability to take a step back, identify your feelings, and rationally address the issues causing your emotional discomfort.

- **Managing The Emotions Of Other People:** Similarly, emotional intelligence helps you identify and understand the emotions of other people, enabling you to better manage their emotions as well.

- **Earning And Receiving Trust:** Build a foundation of trust based on honesty, understanding, and empathy.

- **Better Communication:** Learn how to better say what you really mean, how to be a good listener, and really hear what your partner is saying. Get better at asking good questions or otherwise respond to what your partner's saying in a way that moves the conversation along in a positive and productive direction. Give and receive feedback in a way that's fair and palatable.

- **Negotiate Successfully:** Improve how you cooperate and compromise with your partner, learning how to better offer what they want to get what you need in return.

The list could go on and on. There are almost endless ways that a higher EQ can help you improve your relationship. The question is, how do you do improve it?

Emotional Intelligence And Relationships That Can't—Or Shouldn't—Be Saved

It's important to note, and for you to realize, that not every relationship can be improved or saved. Relationships take the participation, commitment, and emotional intelligence of both partners to work.

It doesn't even necessarily have to be an exact 50/50 split of work between both partners, but if one person is not contributing enough emotionally to the relationship, it will not last. No matter how great your level of emotional intelligence and your mastery of this book, there will be some relationships that you cannot—or should not—save.

When talking about the value of emotional intelligence and the strategies that can be applied to it, this book will advise with the goal to strengthen or improve relationships. In part, this is for simplicity's sake, and it's also because it's the point of the book.

It would be too complicated and confusing to go back and forth between detailing all the ways emotional intelligence can help you improve your relationships, and also the ways those same skills can help you identify and exit bad relationships. The book would become too long, disorganized, and diluted in its goal of helping you strengthen your relationship.

However, much of the information in this book—specifically the portions devoted to improving your self-awareness, self-regulation, social awareness, and social regulation—will also help you identify and exit bad relationships.

How (And Why) Emotional Intelligence Is Taught

Emotional intelligence can be taught because it has components of being a flexible mental characteristic. Flexible mental characteristics are traits or abilities that you can consciously improve or change, as opposed to rigid mental characteristics, which solidify in early childhood and don't change much after that. Some examples of flexible mental characteristics are:

- **Linguistic Ability:** Through study and practice, you can learn new languages or gain a deeper understanding of one you currently speak, increasing your ability to communicate and what would be considered your linguistic intelligence.

- **Logic And Reasoning:** Logic has a long history of formal study, in both philosophy and science. These materials can teach you techniques that improve your logical reasoning ability, such as how to spot classic logical fallacies and how to apply logic to problem-solving. By mastering this knowledge of logic, you'll improve your logical intelligence and reasoning ability.

- **Coordination And Reflex:** Your physical abilities are considered part of your intelligence too. By practicing a specific physical motion—swinging at a baseball, juggling, hitting a speed bag—you improve your hand-eye coordination and reflexes, or "physical intelligence."

Emotional intelligence is like these mental characteristics, in that with practice and study, you can improve. This book is your key to doing so.

How This Book Will Help You Achieve Higher, Everyday Emotional Intelligence

Whether it's linguistics ability or emotional intelligence, the keys to improving any flexible mental characteristic are study, understanding, and practice. This book will give you everything you need to understand every facet of your emotional intelligence—from how you think about yourself to how you emotionally relate to other people—and give you simple strategies, tools, and habits to make the improvements you need to have the relationships you want.

This book is dedicated to everyday improvements in your emotional intelligence, meaning we're not digging deep into the emotional weeds or providing technical background for graduate students. We're focused on giving you practical, actionable information that you can use to make changes to your everyday life. It's through this simple, practical information that you'll be able to make real, noticeable improvements in your relationships.

Excited? You should be! Just ahead, on the next few pages, are your keys to building a greater, more effective understanding of emotion, and using that understanding to improving your current and future relationships.

JAMIE BRYCE

CHAPTER 2:

WHAT IS EMOTIONAL INTELLIGENCE, AND HOW CAN YOU USE IT TO IMPROVE YOUR RELATIONSHIPS?

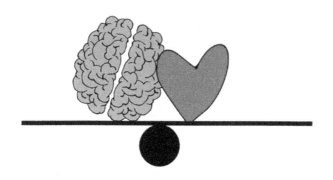

JAMIE BRYCE

Before we dive into the strategies for improving your emotional intelligence, you should be made aware of some background information on emotional intelligence. While there's nothing especially technical in future chapters, some historical background, and context, as well as some terminology definitions, will help deepen your understanding of emotional intelligence as a whole, and also eliminate any possible areas for confusion.

A Short History Of Emotional Intelligence

The term and concept of emotional intelligence first started appearing as a modern psychological concept in the mid-1960s, appearing in psychotherapy journals such as *Practice of Child Psychology* and *Child Psychiatry*. While this makes emotional intelligence a much younger idea than other intelligence measures like IQ, which started appearing in the early 1900s, it still gives emotional intelligence almost 60 years of scientific development. So while it may seem like a new idea by some standards, it's been researched enough to become a solidified concept in psychology.

This is important to note because the terminology and tactics that you'll review later in the book are all backed by real scientific research and study. Emotional intelligence is not "pop psychology," nor is it an idea so new that the psychological science community is still debating its validity. (An example of the latter would be smartphone addiction and its effects on social behavior, something so new and complex that scientists are still trying to come to a consensus on the issue.)

What drove the initial definitions of emotional intelligence was a desire to define and describe aspects of intelligence that weren't covered by "traditional" intelligence measurements, such as IQ tests. By the 1960s, IQ tests were an established tool in the psychological community, and as a result of that establishment, scientists were starting to look at the information provided by those tests and wonder just how complete it really was. IQ tests measured mental abilities like reasoning and problem-solving in a very dry, academic way. Could it be possible that problem-solving in relationships was an entirely different skill than solving an algebra problem?

Compounding this doubt in traditional intelligence testing was the rise of the study of personality in psychology. In psychology, personality is sort of the counterpart to intelligence—if intelligence is what you can do with your mind, personality is how your mind is.

Shyness, conscientiousness, agreeableness, these are all traits a person's mind can have. They don't really have anything to do with intelligence, and therefore would not be defined or studied by an IQ test, or any other measurement of intelligence. Instead, they describe elements of how a person is likely to act in a given situation. (How shyly will they approach meeting a new person? How likely are they to seek out new sensations or experiences? etc.)

The rise of personality psychology was important for the birth of emotional intelligence because it helped show that IQ and other traditional measures of intelligence were not a perfect system for describing someone's mental performance abilities. There were outside reasons for a person's success and/or failure at a task other than how smart they were. Maybe they were too shy to ask questions, maybe they were too extroverted and therefore too busy talking to new friends rather than paying attention to the directions for a task, etc.

Modern personality psychology began in the 1920s, with the publication of Carl Jung's *Psychological Types*, which laid out core personality psychology concepts such as introversion and extroversion. Jung, a student of Freud, is considered one of the founding fathers of modern psychology. His work in personality psychology created a lot of excitement and credibility behind the idea. By the 1950s, scientists had expanded on his ideas, creating the more familiar and complete personality theories such as Myers-Briggs Type and Type A and Type Personalities, which were conceived in the late 1940s and early 1950s.

It's in this crucible that the idea of emotional intelligence is born. By the 1960s, when the idea of emotional intelligence first starts appearing, psychologists are not only thinking about traditional intelligence testing and how it doesn't provide a complete explanation of behavior, they're also seeing personality theory develop and show a whole new spectrum for describing and defining a person's mental traits.

Unlike intelligence, which is considered to be a flexible mental trait, these emerging personality traits were considered rigid, meaning that someone's intelligence could increase or decrease for a variety of reasons, but personality would remain largely unchanging over the course of a person's life. A shy person may become less so over time, or learn ways to cope with and move past their shyness when necessary, but for the most part, a shy person will remain shy for their entire life.

While personality psychology provided a new way to describe and predict human behavior, it still wasn't what those looking for a way to describe emotional intelligence were looking for. The inflexibility of personality traits made them ill-suited for describing emotional intelligence. Because, while you could describe parts of someone's emotional intelligence as traits (how introspective they are, how much empathy they have), doing so doesn't really describe the action of emotional intelligence, which as we'll see in later chapters, is a crucial component of EI.

So, those who were studying emotional intelligence kept looking and working on their own ways to discuss, define and describe the concept in terms that made sense for it. By 1983, there was a legitimate breakthrough: *Frames of Mind: The Theory of Multiple Intelligences* was published by Howard Gardner.

Gardner, a prominent developmental psychologist at Harvard University, provided in the book several new descriptions for different kinds of intelligence that were not covered by traditional intelligence tests, such as musical-rhythmic and bodily-kinesthetic intelligence. These definitions represented the first real time that different kinds of intelligence were laid out as distinct identities.

And while it's true that emotional intelligence was not included as its own identity in Gardner's theory (it instead existed as a combination of several of his categories, including verbal-linguistic, interpersonal, and intrapersonal) his categorical requirements for different kinds of intelligence laid the key groundwork that would later be necessary for defining emotional intelligence.

To prove the existence of the new kinds of intelligence he was describing, Gardener created eight categorical requirements for his new intelligences:

- Can be isolated or destroyed by brain damage

- Has a place in evolutionary history

- Is present in the core operations of the mind

- Can be coded as a programmed task for a computer

- Has a clear developmental progression

- Prodigies and savants exist within the area, e.g., musical geniuses, natural athletes, etc.

- Empirical support from experimental psychology

- Empirical support from psychometric findings.

This was key to the development of the theory of emotional intelligence, especially because for the first time, some of the characteristics on his list defined intelligence as an action and as something that can be learned and improved upon.

After Gardener's multiple intelligences theory, the concept of emotional intelligence continued to gain momentum, appearing in more publications and journals as the years progressed. By 1989 or so, the term "emotional intelligence quotient" ("EQ") was seeing use in psychological journals. In 1995, emotional intelligence had its breakout year, when Daniel Goleman published *Emotional Intelligence—Why It Can Matter More Than IQ.*

The publication of the book is widely credited with popularizing and solidifying the foundation of emotional intelligence in modern psychological theory. Goleman, a longtime science journalist for *The New York Times*, combined much of the research of the time with new analysis to create one of the most popular and widely used theories of emotional intelligence.

The book is dense and full of valuable ideas for the

understanding of emotional intelligence, but for the purposes of this book, there are three contributions from it that are absolutely vital for learning how to improve your own emotional intelligence:

1. **The Idea Of "Emotional Competencies" Which Are Emotional Skills That Are Not Innate, But Can Be Taught, Practiced, And Improved.** This is important because these emotional competencies get into the details of how emotional intelligence can actually be improved, and further establishing the ideas that emotional intelligence is not purely an innate trait that is gifted out at birth, with some people being born "emotionally intelligent," and others less so. It's something that can also be worked on and improved (to a degree) regardless of any EQ levels.

2. **The Idea That Emotional Intelligence Can (And Should) Be Both Measured As A Group Of Abilities And As A Group Of Traits.** Goleman's book sets emotional intelligence up as both an ability and a trait— meaning it's both a traditional form of intelligence that is active and can grow and change, *and* a trait similar to a personality that different people may have different levels of. It may seem like a small distinction, but as we saw in our earlier discussion of the history of

emotional intelligence, the point of flexibility vs. rigidity is an important one. By framing emotional intelligence as both a set of intellectual abilities and a set of personality traits, Goleman not only gave emotional intelligence a much more accurate definition, he provided it a much larger practical range for real-life applications, such as leadership training or relationship improvement.

For example, self-awareness is considered a key component of emotional intelligence. If you only classify self-awareness as an ability, you're defining it as something you do, like running or painting. And like running or painting, self-awareness can be something you can practice to get better at, or conversely, neglect and get worse at. While this is a valuable classification when thinking about improving self-awareness, it ignores a whole other component of self-awareness—some people seem to naturally have more of it than others.

It's important to also be able to think about self-awareness as a trait because it allows us to acknowledge that some people seem to innately have more than others. This is helpful when thinking about your own self-awareness, but the true value of this framing is in thinking about other people. As you work on your own emotional intelligence, you'll also grow to better see the emotional intelligence of other people, and see a range of abilities across many categories, including self-awareness.

3. **The Five Key Subcategories Of Emotional Intelligence.** Goleman described the five foundational subcategories as self-awareness, self-regulation, empathy, motivation and social skills. These subcategories are invaluable in thinking about and framing emotional intelligence because it breaks up the idea into procedural components. Meaning, the first step of higher emotional intelligence is getting better at analyzing and understanding your own behavior, i.e., becoming more self-aware.

   Then, once you have this better sense of self-awareness, you can use it to move onto the next procedural step of higher emotional intelligence, self-regulation. These procedural steps are so important because they provide context and defined targets for improving your emotional intelligence. You're not just trying to become emotionally smarter, you're trying to become more self-aware, have more self-control, to understand others better, etc.

In our book, the last bullet is the most important. Defining the procedural subcategories of emotional intelligence makes it much easier to analyze and teach, and as we'll see in later chapters, also forms the backbone of this book.

Since Goleman's book was published, the study of emotional intelligence has boomed, resulting in a large field of devoted psychological study. There have been some changes and developments to the theory of emotional intelligence since then.

The most notable of which is that most emotional scientists have condensed Goleman's five categories into four*. It's these four subcategories of emotional intelligence that we will use to lay the groundwork for improving your emotional intelligence.

Each of the four subcategories will be better defined in its own chapter, but short definitions of each are as follows:

Self-Awareness: Your ability to understand and "see" your emotions.

Self-Regulation: Your ability to control your emotions and behaviors, both internally (how you feel) and externally (how you present your emotions to other people).

Social Awareness or Empathy: Your ability to "put yourself in others' shoes" and understand the emotions, motivations, and perspectives of other people.

Social Regulation or Relationship Skills:
Your ability to successfully manage your relationships.

Today, emotional intelligence is studied and taught all over the world. It has become an important and thriving area of psychological research, and has also become an effective and valuable avenue for self-improvement. People work to improve their emotional intelligence for a whole host of reasons, from making their relationships better, to increasing performance in the office, to helping with raising a child, to just sleeping better at night.

Now that you've received a basic background in the history and definition of emotional intelligence, we'll move on to how it can actually be built.

*Motivation: The Emotional Intelligence Category Dropped From Goleman's Theory

The subcategory cut from Goleman's five subcategories of emotional intelligence is motivation. Defined as your drive to succeed, there is no doubt that motivation is at least partially an emotional trait. However, there are several reasons motivation is excluded from modern conversations about emotional intelligence.

- **It's not purely an emotional trait.** If you're hungry, it would be reasonable to say you're motivated to eat. If you're tired, it would be reasonable to say you're motivated to sleep. But being tired and hungry are physical demands, and you would classify the motivations that stem from them as physical as well. Similarly, you may be motivated to make money, because you know you need it to live in society. This would be a conscious or practical demand, and motivations that stem from it would be considered practical as well. So, unlike the other four key traits, motivation does not exist purely in the realm of emotional intelligence.

- **It's difficult to define as a fundamental trait.** It can be argued that what we define as emotional motivation is really a combination of other more fundamental personality traits, like self-confidence (*I believe I can achieve things*), self-worth (*I deserve to have the things I need and want*) and imagination (*I can imagine things that I don't have, but want*). So, if you were trying to study or improve your motivation, you'd be better off studying these three components of motivation, rather than motivation alone. The other key components of emotional intelligence, such as self-awareness, are more fundamental traits, meaning that you can't really break them up into other, smaller traits.

- **It's encompassed by the other four subcategories.** Social regulation, social awareness, self-regulation, and self-awareness each contain elements of motivation. Self-awareness and self-regulation tell you why you want to do things, and how to control those feelings, while social awareness and social regulation allow you to do the same, but for others. So, in this way, the motivation category sort of repeats the information presented in the other four categories, without presenting any new perspective or ideas.

- **It's a trait worthy of scientific study, but not one that's very valuable when discussing self-improvement.** When we're talking about self-improvement, it's not very helpful to talk in-depth about motivation, as we will with the other traits. For one, if you're reading a book with the desire to improve yourself, you're probably already pretty motivated. Secondly, motivation is not especially teachable. While there are technically many exercises and strategies you can utilize to boost your self-confidence, energy levels, and self-esteem, doing those things requires motivation, so the whole exercise becomes somewhat silly, circular, and more about raising confidence and self-esteem, rather than motivation. Meaning, even if motivation has a place among the other four categories of EI, it wouldn't have much value to you personally.

JAMIE BRYCE

.

Like what you see so far?

Please **leave a review on Amazon**

letting us know!

CHAPTER 3:

HOW TO BUILD EMOTIONAL INTELLIGENCE AND PUT WHAT YOU BUILD INTO PRACTICE

So now that you know what emotional intelligence is, it's time to get to the fun part— how we build it up and use it to improve your relationships. To build emotional intelligence, you need to learn how to identify areas where you can personally improve, then how to make those improvements. But first, let's talk a little about what you should expect your emotional intelligence improvements to actually look and feel like.

What Growth In Emotional Intelligence Does (And Does Not) Feel Like

In the previous chapters, we talked about how emotional intelligence is both a measure of ability(what you're able to do with your emotional intelligence), and a measure of a trait or how much emotional intelligence you innately have as a person. Abilities are flexible which we can practice and improve, and traits are rigid attributes that are fundamental to our personality. In improving emotional intelligence, you can always improve your emotional intelligence abilities but do not expect to change your emotional intelligence traits.

Think of it this way, if someone has a bad temper, there's a lot they can do to combat it. They can remove themselves from an environment that may make them frequently angry, they can take anger management courses, they can take up meditation, etc. But, even if this person makes great strides in reducing their anger problem, they will always carry that core of a bad temper in their personality.

The same can be said of the trait components of emotional intelligence. You may make massive improvements to your emotional intelligence abilities, but in spite of that, your emotional intelligence traits are unlikely to change.

You might feel like the person in the anger management example. On one hand, the person successfully managing their anger problems feels much better. They feel happier, calmer, and most importantly, a sense of control over their emotions and their behaviors. But on the other hand, they don't feel like an entirely new person either. They can still feel their anger lurking in them, and know they're going to have to work every day to keep making progress, because their inherent personality trait of having a bad temper has yet to go away, and may not ever.

So don't expect to work on your emotional intelligence to feel like a magic cure-all. You're not going to read this book, implement the strategies and tips inside it, and become a completely new person. Certainly, you'll make great improvements, and some of those improvements will be life-changing. But remember that some components of emotional intelligence are rigid traits, and even if you learn to control and work around them, they may never change, nor should you expect them to.

All of us are born and raised with all kinds of different personality traits, at all kinds of different levels. It's a fact of life, well established by personality and emotional intelligence research. The goal of this book is to teach you how to identify who you are emotionally—both from an ability and trait standpoint, and teach you how to work with who are so you can make the relationship improvements you want.

For example, a shy person may never be able to stop being shy, but they can take steps to combat their shyness and finally talk to someone they're captivated with. Further, they can keep beating their shyness and forge a real lasting relationship with that person. So while it's not really possible to change your emotional traits, you can absolutely learn how to work around them and create the life for yourself that you actually want.

Finding The Areas Where You Can Improve Your Emotional Intelligence

To locate the areas where you can improve your emotional intelligence, we're going to take a bottom-up approach. We're going to focus on understanding and improving the fundamental building blocks of emotional intelligence, then work our way up to addressing specific problems and/or areas where you can improve.

The reason for this bottom-up approach is that by focusing on the fundamentals, you'll be creating knowledge, tools, and strategies that can help you improve any and all areas of emotional intelligence you may want to, whether it's how to communicate better, how to trust your partner, or anything else you may want to improve in your relationships.

The alternative to this bottom-up approach is to look at your relationship problems from a top-down perspective, meaning you start with the problem and try and find a solution for it. This approach is inferior to the bottom-up strategy, because you may not be identifying your problem correctly, or seeing the whole picture.

For example, say you're having trouble communicating with your partner, so you start to search for communication advice in relationships. While you find an excessive amount of advice, your communication problem never resolves completely. This is because you may not have just a communication problem, you may have a communication, trust, self-awareness, and anger management problem. Because you approached solving your problems from top-down, you only identified the communication problem, but left the others unsolved—or they may even worsen.

A bottom-up strategy focuses on teaching the fundamentals of emotional intelligence. It avoids the aforementioned problem by giving you the ability to see the whole picture of your relationship—what the problems are, the strengths are, and what you can do to improve things by improving the foundations of both your emotional intelligence and your overall relationship.

The Four Components Of Emotional Intelligence And Why They Form The Foundation Of Improving Your Relationships

As mentioned in earlier chapters, the four components of emotional intelligence are:

> **Self-Awareness:** Your ability to understand and see your emotions.

> **Self-Regulation:** Your ability to control your emotions and behaviors, both internally (how

you feel) and externally (how you present your emotions to other people).

Social Awareness: Your ability to put yourself in others' shoes and understand the emotions, motivations, and perspectives of other people. This is commonly referred to as empathy.

Social Regulation: Your ability to successfully manage your relationships.

These four key components encompass the entirety of emotional intelligence. Focusing on understanding and mastering these components will give you everything you need to improve your emotional intelligence comprehensively. Improving social awareness gives you the ability to truly understand your emotions, which is invaluable in relationships because it gives an understanding of your motivations and reactions to emotional information.

Once you understand those motivations and reactions, you can then use the next key component, self-regulation, to adapt, control, and guide those emotions in a way that's productive for your relationship goals. Social awareness and social regulation will allow you to do the same for your partner, so you'll better understand them. You'll gain the ability to understand their emotional reactions and motivations for behaviors, and also have the ability to manage and guide those emotions in a positive way for your relationship.

The next four chapters are going to discuss each of these four key components in much greater depth, giving you an understanding of each of the components and their role in relationships. The next chapters will also provide practical strategies you can implement to make improvements to your EI. Note, however, that these are not four separate skills that can be used individually. Each one of the skills is used in unison with the others.

Self-awareness has little value without self-regulation. What good is it to understand yourself, but not understand how to do anything with that understanding? Similarly, how can you self-regulate if you don't understand yourself well enough to know what you're actually regulating? How can you be socially aware if you're not able to understand yourself first? And if you're not able to understand yourself, how can you understand others, let alone learn to manage those relationships?

The four components of emotional intelligence are deeply connected. When reading through the next four chapters, keep that in mind and know that you're not building four different skills to help you improve your emotional intelligence and relationships, but one set of unified skills that will give you a powerful and versatile foundation to address whatever relationship issues you may be facing.

CHAPTER 4:

IMPROVING SELF-AWARENESS

Self-awareness is how well you're able to see your own feelings and understand why you're having them in a given situation. It's considered one half of personal competency, for example, how aware you are of your emotions, and based on that awareness, how well you're able to predict and manage your behavior. (The predicting and managing part of personal competency is called self-regulation, which will be discussed in the next chapter.)

We're starting with self-awareness because it's a fundamental part of EI. By raising your self-awareness to higher levels, you'll make the other emotional intelligence skills much easier to use. This is because a high self-awareness helps you make good choices, helps you identify and use your personal strengths, and keep your emotions from holding you back.

Let's spend a little more time on that last point.

What Does It Mean To Have Your "Emotions Hold You Back"?

We've all been there before—so angry, upset, or even excited that it's as if our emotions have taken over. It's an odd sensation, almost like your rational mind gave up control of yourself, and your emotions have overridden everything. It can feel like you're on autopilot, on cruise control, or like watching a movie of yourself or even dreaming. However you want to describe it, the result is the same—your rational mind is not in control of your actions, your emotions are.

When our emotions take over, that can be a dangerous moment in our relationships, because that's when we do things like:

- Say things we don't mean to achieve goals we don't really want.

- Say something cruel just to hurt our partner's feelings.

- Storm off, slam doors, or otherwise throw childish tantrums.

- Propose or agree to things that we don't really want concerning the status of our relationships ("I think we should take a break," "Let's get engaged," etc.)

Being taken over is referred to as emotional hijacking in most emotional intelligence research. That term describes best what it feels like—your emotions have stolen control over you, against your will, hijacking your thoughts and behavior.

Why self-awareness is so important, and why it's the first of the emotional intelligence components we're discussing, is because it's a key solution to emotional hijacking. By identifying when you're being emotionally hijacked, you'll then be able to use your self-regulation skills in the next chapter to break free from that hijacking and return to a more level and functional emotional state.

How does self-awareness combat emotional hijacking, and how can that help improve your relationship?

What Role Self-Awareness Plays In Relationships

Within the specific context of trying to improve your relationships, your self-awareness skills allow you to identify and understand your feelings on every aspect of the relationship, with a high degree of accuracy. With high self-awareness, your emotional interpretations won't stop at "He/she didn't call me back, so now I feel sad."

You'll be able to take it further and come to more insightful emotional conclusions, such as, "They didn't call me back. That makes me feel a little neglected and unimportant. Overall though, I've been feeling a lot of affection from them lately, so I guess I shouldn't let this one missed call bother me too much. It's probably nothing."

As shown in the example above, this improved awareness has great value on its own, by helping you to react better and more appropriately to emotional information. However, self-awareness is also a critical starting point for the three other key emotional intelligence skills. By improving your self-awareness, you will also gain the ability to control your emotions better, and also improve your ability to understand and cooperate with the emotions of your partner.

What A Person With High Self-Awareness Looks Like

To help you understand what self-awareness is and what it looks like in practice, let's take a look at a hypothetical person, and describe what she looks like to others.

How "Perceptive Paula," Who Has High Self-Awareness, Looks To Her Friends And Partner:

- **Paula is aware of how her tone of voice affects others.** Even when she's feeling angry or sad, Paula stays aware of those feelings and doesn't allow them to reflect in her tone of voice, because she knows that letting her emotions hijack how she sounds can make a conversation go in the wrong direction.

- **She is aware that she can be a pushover sometimes.** Paula knows herself well enough that she's aware she has a subconscious habit of being a bit of a people-pleaser at times— giving in to the demands of others despite wanting something different herself. Because of this awareness, she knows to look out for this people-pleasing behavior and corrects it when necessary.

- **She keeps her mind on the big picture.** Paula knows her long-term goals for her relationship with her partner. She uses this awareness to avoid making sacrifices that might go against those long-term goals, even though they might be beneficial in the short-term. (Examples of negative short-term goals would be agreeing with a partner just to end a fight, or choosing to remain silent and not speak up when she's upset.)

To provide a counter-example of someone with low self-awareness, let's look at another hypothetical person, "Short-Sighted Sally."

How Short-Sighted Sally, Who Has Low Self-Awareness, Looks To Her Friends And Partners:

- **She doesn't realize how her emotions make her seem to other people.** Sally is an excitable and nervous person, and she is not afraid to show it. She's often panicked at work, and worries over every little part of her personal relationships. She lets that worry show in her tone of voice and day-to-day behaviors and doesn't realize how that worry is making her partner feel nervous and defensive in response.

- **She has no idea how frantic she seems.** When Sally gets upset, she tends to spin out into a frantic fit. She has no idea this is an issue, however, instead, thinking she's successfully coping with an overwhelming amount of problems.

- **She blames others for her problems, instead of herself.** Sally has trouble distinguishing whose fault something is, often pushing off and blaming others for a problem, instead of seeing her part in an issue when something didn't go her way.

By looking at these examples of people with high and low self-awareness, we can see just what self-awareness looks like in practice. Sometimes, you can read the definitions of a term over and over, but not really understand it until you see an example for yourself, so hopefully the previous examples provided some additional clarity and understanding.

Strategies For Improving Your Self-Awareness

Here are some practical steps for improving your self-awareness. Remember, self-awareness is all about focusing on you, so get ready to tune in on your feelings and emotions. Don't feel bad or get frustrated if this intense level of introspection is challenging for you—or worse, it makes you anxious or uncomfortable. These kinds of feelings are natural when paying attention to yourself more.

Not everyone has the same natural level of comfort thinking about their own feelings, and that's okay. Maybe you were brought up in a household where thinking about or dwelling on your own feelings was not encouraged. Maybe you've never had a need to think about your feelings before—until you tried to really improve a long-term relationship that's important to you. If any of these situations describe your history of self-awareness, that's perfectly fine, and you have nothing to worry about.

Like physical exercise, improving your emotional intelligence is something almost anyone can do—some just have an ability to initially do so more than others. But also like exercise, the longer you stick with it, the better you'll be. Soon enough, you'll be a regular self-awareness power-lifter, impressing others with your ability to flex and understand exactly what you're feeling and why.

The strategies to follow are by no means the *only* ways you can improve your self-awareness. These strategies were selected because they're:

- **High-impact:** The strategies below are worth your time because they'll help you make big, positive changes in your self-awareness ability.

- **Foundational:** Mastering these specific self-awareness strategies is important because they're necessary skills for making improvements in other areas of emotional intelligence.

- **Distinct**: These strategies are different enough from each other. You get to think about and improve your self-awareness in different ways. It will give you more perspective on yourself, and also more versatile tools to get you there.

One last tip: Remember, these strategies are made to examine yourself, not make changes. Taking action and changing comes in the next chapter, on self-regulation. So don't worry that all you're doing is thinking about yourself—that's exactly what you should be doing at this point.

1. Stop Judging Your Feelings

From early on in our lives, we learn to attach a moral value or judgment to our feelings. "It's bad that I'm angry because angry people are bad people." "It's good that I'm happy because being happy is the point of life."

While there's nothing necessarily wrong with enjoying a good emotion (or feeling guilty about a bad one), placing judgments on our emotions can create an obstacle for our self-awareness. With emotions that are considered good, such as happiness or excitement, it's possible to indulge in them too much, neglecting to think about why you're feeling such positive emotions. The reverse is true for bad emotions. We tend to try and push them down and run from them because we feel guilty, bad, or ashamed for feeling them in the first place.

By removing the good and bad judgments from your emotions, you'll allow yourself to really sit, think about, and see the reasons why you're feeling the emotions you're experiencing. This is crucial for both improving your self-awareness and your relationships, for two reasons:

1. **By understanding the "why" of a feeling, you can make plans on how to practically address an issue.** Are you feeling happy that you got a raise because you're making more

money, or are you happy that you got a raise because it means you're now making more money than your partner? These are two very different scenarios that have starkly different implications about yourself and your relationship. Therefore, it's an important distinction to understand.

2. **Suspending judgment of your emotions allows them to run their course.** Worrying about whether you should or shouldn't be feeling something just adds more feelings on top of the emotion in question and prevents you from moving on and properly self-regulating your emotion.

Example: If you're beating yourself up about feeling attracted to someone other than your partner, if also attaching judgment to that sentiment, you're adding guilt and shame on top of your current feeling and perpetuating the thoughts of attraction in your head. By suspending judgment, on the other hand, you allow the emotion to move into the self-regulation phase. You simply do nothing about the attraction, which helps your current relationship and allows you to move on with your day.

The next time you're reflecting on a feeling, avoid

judging it. Instead, think about why you're feeling that way, and what it says about your current relationship or your current place in your life.

2. Pay Attention To Your Negative Emotions

It can be difficult to reflect upon and think about your negative emotions. After all, they're called negative for a reason. No one likes to feel jealousy, shame, anger and all the rest, but sometimes those emotions offer the key to the most rewarding personal improvements and personal growth.

The truth is that negative emotions often indicate a problem in our relationships or our lives. We like to avoid feeling them and thinking about them, because doing so causes us pain, but by doing that, we also cheat ourselves out of the opportunity to identify problems and find solutions.

Pay attention to your negative emotions and take them for what they are—an opportunity to make your life and your relationships better. It may be painful at first, but the more you do it, the more accustomed you'll become to moving past the pain and on to what you really want—a better relationship.

Practical Tip:

Try keeping a journal of your emotions. When first focusing on your self-awareness, whether it's on negative emotions or any kind, it can be helpful to keep a journal of your feelings. Writing things down can help you crystallize your ideas, and also take the sting out of negative emotions to make addressing them easier. Journaling is also a terrific memory tool, helping you become much more self-aware faster.

3. Don't Let Your Current Mood Control You

It's no secret that moods—good or bad—can cloud and control our emotions. When you're in a bad mood, everything seems rotten. Your partner doesn't understand you, you don't have fun anymore, and they're probably going to leave you soon for someone better. Similarly, when you're in a good mood: you and your partner are perfectly in sync, every second you spend together is a joy, and you're going to be together forever.

You can see that being steered by either good or bad moods can be problematic to true awareness of your emotions and the actual state of your relationship. To avoid being steered by your moods, try doing the following:

- Acknowledge that you're in a mood, that it's affecting how you see your relationship, and that it will eventually pass.

- Avoid making any big decisions while in a mood.

- Think about how you got in that mood in the first place.

4. Learn Your Triggers

Everyone has things they find especially upsetting, exciting, or even distracting. This category of stimuli is broadly defined as triggers, and these are things that set us off toward an emotional hijacking.

For you, maybe it's when your partner forgets to put away the dishes or has a loud phone conversation right next to you when you're trying to read, or when they talk over you in an argument. Whatever your triggers are, it's important to be aware of them, because being aware of them is what will allow you to control them and improve your behavior.

When learning and identifying your triggers, you must be as specific as possible. You need to identify the exact people and situations that are triggers for you because this will allow you to focus in on exactly what the issue is, which will allow you to maximize your self-awareness.

For example, say you absolutely despise your ex, Julie Jerkface. Every time you see her post on Facebook, you feel your blood boil in anger. It's not enough for you to say, "Wow, I really hate Julie. Every time I see her post, I'm overcome with rage." You should also think about what she's doing (posting on Facebook) and why it's so infuriating to you. (Perhaps, it's always pictures of her out to brunch with her friends, and when you were dating, you always wanted to go to brunch with her, but she always preferred to sleep in instead.)

By analyzing your triggers further, you can understand why certain situations are so upsetting. Taking the above example further, perhaps missing out on brunch was so upsetting to you not only because it was a source of conflict between you and Julie, but also because you grew up in a big family, and were often left out of lunch and dinner plans with your older siblings, which is something that's always bothered you since.

5. Connect With Your Physical Side

Steps one through four focus on building up self-awareness by identifying and intellectualizing your emotions, but there's another way to feel them—literally. Sometimes, the best way to get in touch with your feelings is to, well, feel them.

Emotions are paired with physical sensations. (That's why they're called feelings after all.) The next time you're feeling a strong emotion—be it happiness, anger, sadness, or anything else—try and focus on the physical sensation of the emotion. Is your body tingling in anger? Are your palms sweating with nervousness? Are your legs shaking with nervousness?

By focusing on your physical reactions, you're improving your ability to connect an emotion with a clear clue that defines the feeling. This physical clues often pop up before mental realizations do, so being connected with the physical side of your emotions can be a great way to give yourself a self-awareness edge.

Improving your self-awareness is your first step toward taking your emotional intelligence and relationships to the next level. By learning how to better identify your emotions and their causes, you give yourself more opportunity to control and guide your actions, through a process referred to as "self-regulation." You also lay the foundation for other emotional skills, such as social awareness, and social regulation, which will be discussed later.

CHAPTER 5:

BETTER SELF-REGULATING

Now that we've talked about self-awareness, it's time to talk about the other part of personal competency: self-regulation.

Self-regulation is your ability to take the emotional information you get from self-awareness and put it into practice, using it to steer your emotions and behavior in the direction you want to. It's the performance part of personal competency and is what actually lets you break out of emotional hijacking and regain control of your actions.

It's important to note though, that self-regulation is more than breaking out of an emotional hijacking. It also has a long-term role in emotional intelligence and healthy relationships. Besides helping you do things like control your tone of voice in an argument, self-regulation also helps you stay on track with long-term goals and avoid short-term behaviors that could damage or derail those goals. An example of short-term behaviors that self-regulation can help you avoid would be selfish actions like frivolous spending, lashing out over trivial problems, and even cheating.

So, self-regulation is important to improving relationships in two key areas: It's how we break out of emotional hijacking, and it's also how we avoid smaller damaging or destructive behaviors and stay on track for long-term relationship goals. The latter point is important and is often where you'll see the best results in your relationships.

What A Person With High Self-Regulation Looks Like

Like we did with self-awareness, let's look at some examples of hypothetical people with high and low self-regulation.

Let's start with "Calm Chris," who has high self-regulation:

- **In an argument, Calm Chris always appears to be patient.** Even in the most heated fights, Chris is able to keep his emotions in check and communicate in a calm, patient way.

- **Chris does not let emotions rule his behavior.** Whether he's sad, angry, or even excited, Chris does not let his emotions guide the way that he acts. He stays focused on his long-term personal and relationship goals and acts in a way that would benefit them, regardless of his current feelings.

- **Chris controls his impulses for sarcasm.** Chris has a dry sense of humor and likes to tease people in a way that sometimes comes off as too sarcastic or rude. But, he knows this behavior can not only be hurtful, but put his relationships at risk, so he resists the temptation to make these jokes and rarely lets any slip.

Now, let's look at a counter-example of someone with low self-regulation, "Impulsive Ivan."

What low self-regulation looks like, with Impulsive Ivan:

- **Ivan lets his emotions rule in an argument.** Any which way an argument is going, that's how Ivan will be. If he's mad, he's yelling. If he's sad, he's crying. He lets his emotions completely dictate his behavior in a fight, often to disastrous results.

- **How Ivan feels dictates what he does.** If Ivan is feeling sad, he'll push loved ones away. If he's happy or lonely, he'll try to draw his partner closer. There's no reasoning for his actions beyond how he feels. No plan, no thought, just the feelings of the moment guiding his behavior, which often leaves his partner feeling confused and frustrated.

- **Impulsive Ivan is, well, impulsive.** Ivan has a lot of trouble in managing his short-term wants versus his long-term goals. He often spends more money than he should, just to get something he wants right now. He makes, then cancels or changes plans on a whim. He flirts with ex-lovers and colleagues without any regard for long-term consequences to his current relationship.

Strategies For Improving Your Self-Regulation:

Here are some practical steps for improving your self-regulation, allowing you to utilize the knowledge you've gained from your improved self-awareness. These are the strategies that let you put all the brand-new self-awareness you've built into action, which means you want to make sure that you have a decent handle on your self-awareness before diving into this section and trying to apply these strategies into your relationships in real life. Otherwise, you may be trying to apply solutions to problems that don't actually exist—which is never where you want to be.

That said, the strategies in this section were picked not only because they're high-impact, foundational and distinct from each other, but also because they work in a complementary way to the self-awareness strategies given in Chapter Four. (This is also probably a good point to mention that the strategies below are of course not the only ways you can learn to self-regulate. There are many, many more out there. The five below were picked because they provide you with the best possible foundation for improving your self-regulation skills.)

By working in a complimentary way, we mean that the better you get at one of the skills, the better you'll get at the other skill. For example, take the first self-regulation skill below: Diffuse negative emotions and impulsiveness by adding time. Certainly, to realize that you're having negative emotions or being impulsive, you need sufficient self-awareness skills.

However, learning to control your negative emotions and impulses will also help you recognize them more. Think of it this way: The first time you use one of these strategies to break out of an emotional hijacking, won't that feel good? And because it feels good, won't you be more likely to realize your negative feelings in the future, and use the same strategy to break out again?

Like with self-awareness, don't worry if self-regulation doesn't come easily to you at first. Remember that everyone has different innate levels of all the components of emotional intelligence, and self-regulation is no exception to that. This book—and improving your relationships—are not about where your abilities are right now. It's about how we can take them forward. So take a deep breath, relax, and get ready to improve your self-regulation ability, one step at a time.

1. Diffuse Negative Emotions And Impulsiveness By Adding Time

Whether you're gripped in an especially intense emotional hijacking, or just considering doing something you might regret, time can be the solution.

If you're trapped in an intense emotional hijacking, try counting to ten. It may seem silly or absurd, but there's an effective truth in the old method of counting to calm down. By forcing your brain to shift gears into something else, you'll force your mind to switch and focus on a different kind of task—one that's much more rational and disconnected from whatever you're feeling. You may not make it all the way to ten, but shifting your attention to such a different task kind of has the effect of splashing your face with cold water—it's a soft reset and frees you from whatever you're feeling at the moment.

Counting to ten isn't the only way time can work in your favor and help you control your emotions. If you're struggling with a difficult emotional choice, whether it's an impulsive decision you know you shouldn't do, or simply a difficult emotional choice that you're having trouble wrapping your head around, often times the best way to ensure you make the right choice is to sleep on it.

Sometimes, a particular emotional situation or relationship is so frustrating or painful, our first impulse is to make a decision immediately, just to alleviate the pain. But doing so often means letting our emotions make the choice, not our minds, which can lead to decisions we regret down the road. Instead, it can often be better to let your emotions settle and reset after a night's sleep. Usually, six-to-eight hours of sleep is enough to repress any reckless impulses or to allow enough time to pass to allow your rational mind to catch up with your emotional desires.

Practical Tip: How To Sleep Better

Sometimes when we're emotionally hijacked, sleeping on a decision is easier said than done. Your mind is racing, you can't get comfortable, and you're waking up every couple hours with the same worries or unwelcome thoughts, over and over. Thankfully, there are lots of things you can do to improve your nightly rest, from daily exercise to the overall improvements to emotional intelligence you'll gain from this book. Here are a few quick and easy things you can do to set yourself up to sleep better:

- **Avoid caffeine in the afternoon and evening.** Caffeine stays active in your body for an extremely long time, taking approximately 12 hours to fully pass from your body. This means that even a post-lunch cup of Joe can have an effect on your ability to sleep. A recent article in *Psychology Today* stated that caffeine consumed 6 hours before sleeping will reduce your overall sleep time by 1 hour, as well as significantly increasing the amount of time spent awake during the night. So if you want to sleep better, cutting back on the coffee is key.

- **Get outside for at least 20 minutes in the morning.** Morning sunlight is important for calibrating your internal clock and therefore putting yourself on a regular sleep schedule, so do what you can to get outside for a bit in the morning. It doesn't have to be sunny, and it doesn't have to be 20 continuous minutes, but it can't be filtered through windows or glass. So whether it's rolling down your car windows, waiting in the open air on the train platform, or taking your dog for a short walk in the morning, do what you can to spend a little time outside in the a.m.

- **Stay away from electronic screens for about two hours before going to sleep.** Similar to how the morning sun calibrates your internal clock for sleep, electronic screens can have the opposite effect. Bright screens like your TV, computer, and smartphone can make your body think it's a different time of day than it actually is, which can prolong your wakefulness and keep you from settling into an easy sleep. If you're someone who likes to browse their phone at night, note that while features like night mode that are designed to reduce the light output of your phone do in fact make it less bright, there are no scientific studies as of yet that verify if they actually reduce the harm done to your sleep or not.

2. Control How You Talk To Yourself

Regulating your self-talk, i.e., getting the voice inside your head to talk to you in the right way, is a critical component of your self-regulation. Research suggests that you have tens of thousands of thoughts every day, many of which are spoken to you by your internal voice. Sometimes, that voice does not talk to us in a way that's beneficial to regulating our emotions.

"Why did I do that? I'm so stupid."

"I can't believe I said that. I'm such a loser."

"He's going to leave me because I'm so ugly and boring."

Most of us have had thoughts like these at one point or another, and most of us know how such thoughts can send us into a miserable emotional hijacking, where we just beat ourselves up over and over and over.

Even negative self-talk like the examples above doesn't have to be so brutal. With some slight changes in phrasing, it's possible to smooth over and diminish your negative self-talk, so it's more emotionally manageable. Here are a couple examples of ways to smooth over the most common negative self-talk problems:

- **Instead of "I always" or "I never," say "This time."** While you don't want to ignore any habitual problems you may have, it's important to give yourself a chance to change and acknowledge each success or failure as its own distinct event.

- **Judge the event, not yourself.** We grow up learning to connect success or failures to ourselves, e.g., "I'm a winner because I did this thing right," or "I'm a loser because I did this thing wrong." But, not only is that faulty reasoning (winners also do things wrong sometimes, losers also do things right sometimes), it's misleading because actions are what can be right or wrong, not people. So, when criticizing your past behavior, it's much more accurate and helpful emotionally to say "I made a mistake when I did this," as opposed to "I was an idiot when I did this."

- **Avoid responsibility extremes.** It's important to take responsibility for your feelings and actions, and it's also important to blame others when blame is due, but rarely is it correct to say something is *all* your fault or *all* their fault. Doing so can lead to some particularly frustrating and inaccurate self-talk.

3. Create More Emotional Control By Harnessing The Power Of Positivity

One of the bigger obstacles to effective emotional control is being emotionally hijacked by negative emotions. Negative emotions reduce your motivation to do anything, as well as your belief in your ability to achieve your goals. Think of it this way: You may be able to picture someone who's too caught up in their happiness, but you'd never imagine that person sitting in bed, too afraid and beaten-down to make changes in their lives.

Breaking out of negative emotional hijacking is not always easy, but there are some tricks you can use and habits you can implement to loosen its grip and introduce some positivity into your life:

- **Force a smile.** This one may seem silly, but forcing a smile is scientifically proven to improve your mood. Research shows that even doing things similar to smiling, like holding a pencil in your mouth, is adequate. The smile muscles in your face are closely connected to your emotions of happiness so anything you can do to use them (even if it's holding a pencil in your mouth) can help you improve your mood.

- **Picture yourself succeeding at difficult tasks.** This is old advice, but there's scientific support for its value. MRI scans of people actually watching the sunset versus those just picturing it in their mind are virtually identical, meaning your brain has trouble telling the difference between what you're really seeing and what you're imagining.

The value here is that you can picture yourself completing a difficult task, like having a hard conversation with a partner, as a way of practicing it in your head. If you picture yourself handling the conversation in a calm, positive way, it will help you do so in real life as well.

- **Focus on the immediate tasks at hand.** Sometimes being more positive can seem like a big, overwhelming project, where you're not sure how to start. When this is the case, don't worry about the big picture, focus on the next immediate step, whether that's getting out of bed to exercise, taking some time to write a short gratitude list of things you're thankful for, or even spending some time with some friends. By focusing on the immediate task, you'll find that your mind and body line and up and start focusing on the positive direction you want.

4. Get An Outside Perspective From Someone Else.

We like to think we have all the answers and can solve all our problems on our own—self-sufficiency is an important component of self-confidence after all. But the reality is, especially when we're emotionally hijacked, we can't see all the parts of our problems.

Talking about relationship problems with someone else can seem difficult or embarrassing at first, but it's also one of the most effective ways to break out of an emotional hijacking. By communicating you can get a new perspective and learn how to better regulate your current and future emotions.

We can get so tied up in our own emotions and our own needs, it can be difficult to see our partner's perspective. Talking to someone else who can give you an honest, unbiased, and outside perspective can be a valuable way to escape the emotional tangle of your own needs and desire to defend your side of the story.

When looking for someone to talk to, it's important that you choose someone who is not just going to take your side and tell you what you want to hear. People like your drinking buddy who's always hated your partner, your Mom who believes you can do no wrong, or a coworker you suspect might have a crush on you, are all bad choices.

Choose someone you can trust, someone you're comfortable with, but also someone who's going to be neutral and tell you the truth. Your friend who's known for telling harsh truths, your dad who's never coddled and always pushed you to be better, or ideally, a therapist who's paid to give you honest perspective and feedback are all better options. These are the people you want to bounce your relationship problems off of because they're the ones that are going to give you the truth and perspective you need.

5. Learn To Accept—And Expect—Change

Change can be intimidating, especially when it comes to our relationships. But, to successfully emotionally self-regulate, it's necessary to accept that change is a part of life, and will sometimes come to your relationships even if you don't want it to. To truly regulate your emotions, you need to accept that things can change, because you need to mentally prepare for those changes and think through the emotions and consequences that are going to come from that change. This preparation helps prevent you from getting emotionally hijacked by negative feelings like shame, disappointment, and shock that can pop up and surprise you when a relationship is going through a negative change.

Practical Tip: Write Out A "Coming Changes" Outline

To help yourself prepare for relationship changes that may be on the way, don't just run through them in your head over and over at night. Take your thoughts and planning deeper, and take the time to outline the changes you think might be on the way, and what the consequences of them might be. Then, write out possible solutions for those consequences. Even if these changes never happen, you'll feel better and more in control of your emotions from this preparation exercise.

Improving your self-regulation is a vital part of using your improved self-awareness and higher emotional intelligence to improve your relationships. When you learn how to better control your emotions, you create positive change in your life and your relationships that will not only improve them on their own but also give you other relationship benefits, such as improved empathy and trust from your partner.

Completing this chapter on self-regulation completes our discussion of personal competency, which is how aware you are of your emotions, and based on that awareness, how well you're able to predict and manage your behavior. The next chapters will deal with social competence, which is your ability to understand other peoples' emotions, behaviors, and motivations and use that information to improve your relationship.

Sharing is caring.

Let other people know that

you like this book and they will too

by **leaving a review on Amazon**!

CHAPTER 6:

SHARPENING YOUR SOCIAL AWARENESS

JAMIE BRYCE

Social awareness (or what you might be more familiar with, empathy) is kind of like your self-awareness— only applied to other people instead of yourself. Social awareness is defined by your ability to accurately identify and understand the emotions of others. Like self-awareness, it's a foundational skill for emotional intelligence, allowing you to advance your relationships in a productive and positive direction.

As one half of the group of emotional skills we refer to as social competencies, social awareness is the half that lets you identify and understand the emotions that might be causing problems. The other half, your relationship management skills, is what allows you to act on this information and make these changes. Like self-awareness and self-regulation, we will discuss relationship management in the next chapter, after we lay out ways you can improve and utilize your social awareness.

What Role Does Social Awareness Play In Relationships?

So far, we've spent a lot of time talking about you in this book. How you feel, why you feel that way, and what you can do to control those feelings and act on them in a way that's beneficial to you and your relationship. However, relationships aren't all about you, how you feel, and what you do. There's a whole other person to think about when we're talking about improving relationships—your partner!

Like how self-awareness works for understanding yourself, social awareness is how you understand your partner. It's how you identify their emotions, see the thoughts behind them, and understand their reasons for feeling that way (even if you don't agree). Also like self-awareness, social awareness is all about listening and observing, only instead of paying attention to yourself, you're paying attention to your partner.

What A Person With High Social Awareness Looks Like:

Let's take a look at a hypothetical person with high social awareness, "Empathetic Elaine," and see what that would mean for her relationships:

- **Elaine can get along with almost anyone.** No matter where Elaine is, or who she's with, she seems to get along well with all people. She fits in at parties, is well-liked in the office, and gets along with her partner's in-laws with relative ease. This is not because she is an amazing or profoundly interesting person, it's because Elaine has a good feel for other people's personalities, and is able to act—and react—in ways these people find pleasant, appropriate and expected.

- **Elaine is good at communicating other people's feelings to a third party.** Elaine is a talented storyteller. One of her best skills is accurately communicating the feelings other people had at the time. Why So-and-So's feelings were hurt, why Steve fell in love with Sally, how Peter felt when he got that big promotion.

- **Elaine is an active listener.** When she is listening to someone talk, Elaine is very engaged. She naturally keeps welcoming body language, follows the course of the conversation well, and asks appropriate and worthwhile questions based on the context and details of the story she's being told.

Now let's look at Elaine's hypothetical counterpoint: Self-absorbed Sandra. Let's see what someone with low social awareness looks like in a relationship.

- **Sandra struggles in new social situations.** When meeting new people or going to a new place, Sandra has trouble fitting in. She struggles to read the tone of a room or setting, and will often act in ways that aren't quite appropriate, creating stress and embarrassment for herself and others.

- **Sandra is a bad listener.** For Sandra, conversations only have two parts: When she gets to talk, and when she doesn't. She always seems to be waiting to express her opinion on a given subject, and what she has to say rarely has much to do with what's being said by the other party.

- **Sandra has a hard time understanding where others are coming from.** Sandra has a rigid understanding of what's fair and unfair and has a very hard time understanding someone who doesn't agree with her. This causes a lot of problems in her current relationship, where she just can't understand why her partner has to talk to their mom so much. (Sandra only talks to her mom once a month. Why would anyone need to talk to a parent more than that?)

Strategies For Improving Your Social Awareness

Here are some strategies and tips for improving your social awareness. When you set out to use these strategies, don't forget about the self-awareness skills you picked up in Chapter Four, because being able to understand yourself is incredibly helpful when trying to understand others. Almost all of the strategies laid out below—from working on your listening skills to learning about your partner's culture and background—can be made much more effective if you're able to use your self-awareness skills to complement them.

For example, take the first strategy described below: Work on your listening skills. To complement that strategy, you can use your self-awareness skills to determine if you're in a good emotional state to be listening right now. Are you attentive and alert, or are you distracted by anger or tiredness or worrying about work? And, if you determine you're not in a good emotional state to listen, then you should use your self-regulation skills and strategies from Chapter Five to see if you can make yourself more ready to listen.

One last tip before proceeding with this chapter: Be aware that some people are just harder to understand than others. While these social-awareness skills are powerful and broadly applicable, they are by no means a perfect and complete solution for understanding other people.

This doesn't mean that if you're not connecting with someone that it's automatically their fault—no one's social awareness is perfect, and it's often reasonable to assume that there's something you can do on your side of the relationship to improve your ability to understand your partner. By saying some people are more difficult to understand than others, it means that: **Your experience and success using these tips can vary from person to person.**

It's somewhat of an obvious point to say, but people are different, and their differences play a role in how you're able to connect with them. Part of social awareness is being able to assess those differences, but it's also important to know that your ability to assess them is not just affected by your own emotional intelligence, but by how transparent or guarded the particular person is.

Some people are very guarded and skilled at hiding their emotions, while others may be generally poor communicators, making it harder for you to listen and connect as well as you'd like. So don't worry if you feel like you've made amazing progress with your social awareness skills, but still find some people difficult to connect with—it could very well be them, and not you.

That doesn't mean that you should give up or write the person off, it just means that you'll have to work that much harder on your own social-awareness skills to connect   with   them.

As with the other sections, the five strategies listed below are not the only avenues for improving your social-awareness. These were selected because of their effectiveness, depth, and range for improving your social awareness.

1. Work On Your Listening Skills

One of the most important components of social awareness is your ability to listen, not just to the words your partner is saying, but how they're saying them. What are they doing with their body? Are their arms folded? Are they gesturing wildly? Did they reach out to hold your hand before talking? What about the tone of their voice? Or the speed they're talking? Are they nervously stuttering? Yelling in anger?

Improving how you pick up on these emotional cues will go a long way toward improving your social awareness. Here are some other things you can do to improve your listening skills:

- **Focus on the conversation:** This is easier said than done for some people, but do your best to listen to the conversation. Try and keep your mind from wandering, and don't worry about what you want to say next. Just keep yourself in the moment and listen to what your partner is saying to you.

- **Ask questions:** During a conversation, don't hesitate to ask questions, no matter how serious the conversation seems. Questions are a great way to increase your understanding of a given situation. Open-ended questions like, *"How did that make you feel?"* can help you gather valuable corroborating information on the situation, which will help you build more empathy and understanding with your partner. Closed-ended questions, like, *"When did this happen?"* can help you slow a conversation down and give you more time to process what's being said and give you valuable details essential to fully understanding the story.

- **Be agreeable and encouraging:** By offering small encouragements throughout the course of a conversation like, "I see your point" or "I see why you'd feel that way," you'll make your partner more comfortable and relaxed in the conversation. Once they're more comfortable and relaxed, they'll communicate more effectively, making your job of listening a whole lot easier.

2. Put Yourself In Your Partner's Shoes

"Put yourself in their shoes" is a common expression with a widely understood meaning: Step into their place and imagine things from their perspective. Next to listening, putting yourself in their shoes is one of the most important ways to increase your social awareness and is the core principal of empathy. It gives you a whole new perspective on the emotions and motivations of your partner, which in turn is invaluable for improving many elements of your relationship.

Sometimes, it can be hard, daunting, or even impossible to put yourself in your partner's shoes— especially if one or both of you are gripped deep in a serious emotional hijacking. "How could they say that?!" "I can't believe she feels that way!" "Why would he do what he did?! It's just insane!"

Take a step back, and take the emotion out of it. Think of putting yourself in their shoes as a game, like solving a puzzle, or like an acting role. Use your imagination, step out of yourself, and try and solve the mystery of your partner's behaviors.

Remember, when you're out of your shoes, and in someone else's, the goal is to think as if you were *them*—not *yourself* in their position. The only way you're going to be able to understand their perspective is if you commit to thinking about things the way they do. Use what you know about their personality, their background, and what you believe them to be feeling to give yourself the best understanding possible of why your partner is acting or feeling the way that they do.

3. Choose The "Right" Moments To Make Your Point

Just like your mood and emotions play a role in how you react to things, so to do your partner's. When you need to bring up something that may cause conflict, it's important that you're able to choose the right moments to do so.

For example, your partner just got in a knock-down, 10-alarm screaming match with her sister. Right after that fight would not be a good time bring up the controversial camping trip you want to take with your drinking buddies and your ex-girlfriend, Sensual Suzanne.

Nor would it be a good time to bring up how your

mother is going to be living with you both for the next couple months. And it would be an especially bad time to point out that your partner needs to calm down, because you're really tired of listening to the complaining, and besides, you think her sister was in the right in the argument anyway.

However, that doesn't mean the above points shouldn't be discussed. They're important issues that should be addressed, they just need to be brought up at the right time, i.e. when your partner is in a reasonable emotional state to participate in a more difficult conversation.

Here are some things you can do to help identify the right moments to discuss difficult moments with your partner:

> **Use your listening skills.** Listen to what your partner is saying, and how they're saying it. Pay attention to other cues like their body language and tone of voice. If it seems like they're not in the mood to have a serious conversation, don't try and force one.

> **Make small talk**. Having a light conversation with your partner can be a practical way to identify their mood. Ask them about their day, about dinner, about your favorite TV show, or the latest gossip in your shared social circle and see how they react. Do they seem engaged? Or

are they disinterested in topics that normally excite them? By feeling out their mood through various conversation subjects, you can get a sense of how ready they could be for a larger conversation.

Put yourself in their shoes. If you know on the surface level why your partner is upset (say for example that you were present for the blow-up fight they had with their sister), then put yourself in their shoes and think about how they're feeling right now.

If you had just a huge fight with your sister, would you be in the right mindset to have a serious conversation? Or would you be so overcome with emotion from the argument, that what you'd need most from your partner is some emotional support and understanding?

4. Learn The Rules Of Your Partner's Cultural And Socioeconomic Background

How and where people are raised affects how they express and interpret emotions. A person born to a rich Catholic family who was raised as an only child is going to have different emotional behaviors compared to someone who grew up in a poor family of seven that never really went to church.

Being able to identify and understand the emotional differences that stem from different upbringing is a core component of social awareness. Why?

Because different upbringing trains people on different emotional and social rules. Even if your partner grew up with a background largely similar to yours, there could still be socioeconomic or cultural factors creating tension in your relationship. A few examples:

- **Your partner is reluctant to move in to your apartment before marriage.** Even though you've been dating for years, they're reluctant to take the next step and move in with you, and they're not really explaining why. At first, you think it's because they're having doubts about your relationship, but then you think about their background a little.

  They grew up in a large, religious family, where every one of their older brothers and sisters got married before moving in with their partners. If they moved in with you before getting married, they'd be the first to go against this tradition, putting them in a potentially awkward situation with their family.

- **Your partner gets upset when they see you throwing away some old food that's gone bad.** You let three-quarters of a bag of vegetables go bad in your fridge. It was an honest mistake, they were just hidden behind some other items, and you didn't see them for a couple weeks. Shrugging it off, you simply threw the vegetables away.

Your partner sees this and lets out a big, disappointed sigh, and maybe even has a few words for you in a not-so-nice tone of voice. You notice this is an unusually intense reaction for a $3.00 bag of vegetables. You think it's because they're the one who paid for the vegetables but thinking about it more, you realize it's because they grew up in a poor family, where food was especially previous, so spoiled food was both rare, and a big deal if it happened.

- **Your partner takes great offense when one of your friends makes an off-hand joke about single moms.** While hanging out at a party, one of your friends makes a passing joke about single moms always being in their kids' business. Your partner jumps down your friend's throat, browbeating him over how hard single moms have it, and how he shouldn't make jokes about things he doesn't understand. While you agree that the joke was dumb, you also don't think it warranted such an intense reaction.

You first think your partner reacted that way because they're in a bad mood, and maybe even because you think they don't like your friend (he can be a bit hard to digest sometimes), but then you're able to connect her reaction to her background. Because she grew up with an overbearing single mother, you realize she's probably very sensitive about single mothers, both because she loves her mother and appreciates the things she did for her, but also because she feels some embarrassment, shame, and bitterness over some ways her overbearing mother treated her and doesn't enjoy having people remind her of it, even if it's in a simple passing joke.

The above examples are based on you knowing your partner fairly well, but what if you don't? What if you've only just met, and don't have a firm understanding of their background?

Just ask questions.

It's that simple. Take the time to ask about your partner's background and upbringing. How they grew up, where, what their siblings were like, if their parents got along, all the things you'd want to know to help you understand where they're coming from.

5. Get Opinions On Yourself From Others.

Social awareness isn't just about how you see other people—it's also about how other people see you. Understanding how people see you can not only give you important information on your behavior, it can also give you valuable information on how other people are personally interpreting your behavior.

For improving social awareness, it's the latter point of how others are interpreting your emotions and behaviors that we're talking about. For example, if you feel you come off as calm and fair in arguments, but your partner insists that you come off as condescending and snippy, who's really right?

The likely answer is that both of you are some parts correct, but that's not really a useful answer. To get closer to the truth, you may want to ask close friends how they think you come off in arguments. Do they think you're calm? Or do they think your calmness masks a quiet, sarcastic temperament?

The answer they give will help you determine your next action: If they also think you're a little mean in arguments, then your partner is right, and you need to be nicer in arguments. If the opposite is true, however, then you know that your partner is perhaps more sensitive than your friends, and you can use that information to guide future behavior with them.

Practical Tip: Take An Emotional Intelligence Survey, And Ask Your Friends To Evaluate You As Well.

You can actually send your close friends a survey about yourself that asks them to answer specific emotional intelligence information about yourself. Called 360-degree surveys, they're easy enough to find online. You can even take the quiz yourself, and compare your answers about yourself to what your friends say. (Often, your friends' answers turn out to be much more accurate than your own!)

Improving your social awareness is a critical part of increasing your emotional intelligence and understanding your relationships in a whole new way. By learning how to better identify the emotions and moods of others, you give yourself more opportunity to adapt to their behaviors and needs, through the final component of emotional intelligence broadly referred to as social regulation or relationship skills, which will be discussed in the following chapter.

CHAPTER 7:

STEPPING UP YOUR SOCIAL REGULATION

The fourth and final component to improving your emotional intelligence is social regulation—your ability to use the information you're getting from both your self-awareness and your social awareness to successfully manage your relationships. This component of emotional intelligence is also sometimes referred to as social skills or relationship management. For the purposes of this book, however, we'll be using the term "social regulation" to match with its sister term from Chapter Five, self-regulation.

Social regulation is the second half of your social competencies, the first being social awareness. Social regulation allows you to act on the information you've gained from social awareness, in order to improve your relationships. It can also help you free someone from emotional hijacking—only this time the person you're removing is your partner, and not yourself.

Unlike the other three components of emotional intelligence, social regulation fully depends on your abilities in the other three areas—self-awareness, self-regulation, and social awareness. This is because, as you probably now know, to affect change in a relationship, you not only have to understand your partner but also yourself.

Why Social Regulation Is Important To Emotional Intelligence And Improving Your Relationships

Social Regulation is important to your relationships because, in many ways, it *is* your relationship. How you interact, understand, and communicate with your partner is more or less how a relationship is defined. So, while self-regulation, and self- and social-awareness are extremely important to your emotional intelligence and your relationship, social regulation is all about the relationship itself, i.e., how you and your partner are working together to enjoy your time together.

What A Person With High Social Regulation Looks Like:

Let's look at another hypothetical person, and see what high social regulation skills look like in a relation, with "Successful Stan":

- **Successful Stan is understanding.** Everyone who spends time with Stan comes away with the feeling that he understands them. People feel listened to, and also that Stan is legitimately interested in what's going on in their life. He's someone people can talk to about their problems and receive fair advice when they want it, and consolation and support when they don't.

- **Successful Stan is level-headed.** Even in times of stress, Stan seems to keep his cool. His level-head has been very valuable in his relationships, allowing him to have hard conversations and handle bad news with little difficulty or emotional hijacking.

- **Successful Stan has a great marriage.** Stan has been married for over 25 years. While his marriage has had its ups and downs, overall, people describe his relationship with his partner as idyllic. And while Stan's partner would never describe him has perfect, they do feel a very strong sense of connection and trust with him. They may fight now and again, but there are few persistent arguments or long-term problems that cannot be solved.

Now let's look at our last hypothetical person, "Frustrating Frank," and see what low social regulation looks like in a relationship:

- **Frustrating Frank is tough to be around.** Frank has a terrible habit of making every conversation about him. He's a poor listener and struggles to read the mood of the room. He tells jokes at the wrong time, and is constantly talking over, or even yelling at, people to get his opinions heard.

- **Frustrating Frank is moody beyond belief.** Frank seems to have no control of his emotions, and has a habit of letting his feelings steer him down whatever path they happen to lead him down. Even worse, Frank takes his negative emotions out on others, often blaming them for his feelings, even when they're not at fault.

- **Frustrating Frank has a hard time with long-term relationships.** Frank is able to date and meet new people with some success. However, as soon as a relationship hits its first rough patch, Frank is out the door. He seems unwilling, or even unable, to resolve conflict in a way that would preserve his relationships.

Strategies For Improving Your Social Regulation

Let's look at some strategies for improving your social regulation abilities. To do these well, you're going to need your other three emotional intelligence skills, so come prepared!

Some of the strategies in this section are a little longer and more in depth than in the other sections. We're tackling some more complicated strategies in this section, such as having a difficult conversation with your partner. That's because social regulation is where the more complex work gets done in improving relationships.

Think of it this way: Understanding and managing the emotions of one person is difficult on its own (we spent two chapters on it), but adding another person to the situation makes it much more complicated.

That's not to say that it's more difficult—or that you should be worried in any way—just that some of these strategies are inherently more complex than those that appear in the other chapters.

Like with the other three EI skills, don't be put off if you don't immediately adjust to social-regulation. This is undoubtedly the most difficult one of the four components of emotional intelligence to master. Not only does succeeding in it require you to have excellent social awareness, self-regulation, and self-awareness, but it also demands the same from the other person in the relationship! So, it's important to remember that not everyone's emotional intelligence is the same (nor a good match for yours). As a result, some interactions and relationships can be more difficult than others.

But, always remember, difficulty doesn't necessarily mean it's time to give up. Sometimes, you just need to intensify your efforts or try a new approach to make progress with someone you're having a little more trouble connecting with than normal.

Social regulation is an absolutely massive topic, and because of its importance in relationships, has been explored and researched in great depth. The five strategies below are far from the only ways you can approach improving your self-regulation skills.

There is a wealth of information out there on the subject. We selected these five topics for similar reasons as we did for the other three chapters: These strategies are high-impact, foundational skills that will give you a diverse and sturdy foundation for improving your social regulation.

1. In Arguments, Offer Solutions

When you're in the throes of an argument with your partner, sometimes the last thing you want to do is give up on trying to prove you're right and instead offer a solution to the problem your partner is facing. But to improve your emotional intelligence in your relationship, you must be prepared to do exactly this.

Take a step back and think about it this way. Say you're at a fast-food restaurant, and the clerk at the counter has gotten your order wrong and given you the wrong food. You approach the clerk with the wrong order and point out his mistake.

Now, the clerk is pretty positive that your order is correct, and that you just accidentally ordered something you didn't want. However, even if the clerk is positive that is the case—that you really did order wrong—he'll never point that out to you, the customer. Instead, he'll offer a solution—after a quick apology, he'll fix your order and ask the kitchen to make you what you really wanted, free of charge.

Why does the fast food clerk do this? Because who cares who's right or wrong in this situation? The clerk wants to keep you as a customer, and it takes almost no effort or expense to correct the order. Even though the clerk is almost positive that you ordered incorrectly, and he could argue that point if he wanted to, doing so would be counterproductive to his goals of keeping you as a customer and maintaining that relationship.

Now, that is a bit of a simplistic example. Certainly, most relationship arguments are not as simple or low stakes as an argument in a fast-food restaurant. However, two core points from the above example carry over perfectly for relationships:

- **You gain nothing by fighting over who's correct and who's incorrect this very second.** There are exceptions to this rule, but for the most part, "who's right and who's wrong" conversations rarely succeed when they've escalated into full-blown arguments. Instead, all each side really achieves is adding more stress and baggage into a relationship. So if there's nothing to gain besides a small victory for your pride, and there's plenty to lose, why even bother fighting about it?

- **Offering solutions reduces tensions, builds trust, and sometimes ends the argument outright.** After the fast food clerk corrected your order, would you continue to complain to him about the initial order being wrong? Probably not, because what would be the point?

Now, the solution you offer may not be as complete and cut-and-dry as a fixed food order, but applying the same principle can lead to similar results. For example, if you're fighting about your weekend plans, you could offer to spend time with your partner's family this weekend, and let them know that next weekend, you'd like to go out with your friends. After all, does it really matter who's right about where your social time should be spent, if you're both getting something you want out of the solution?

2. Have The Tough Conversations

We've alluded to tough conversations throughout this book. Now that we've built up some emotional intelligence tools, it's time to talk about how to actually have them. Here are some strategies you can use to make your touchy conversations easier to have, smoother to experience, and ending with better emotional results for both you and your partner.

Start On Common Ground.

Tough conversations tend to go better if you and partner begin from a point of agreement. It builds a sense of trust and involvement, helping your partner feel like you're both on the same team, and also that you have shared stakes in the conversation.

Sometimes a common ground is easy to find ("*We both know our relationship has been struggling for a little while*" or "*You know that I love you*"). But that's not always the case. If you're struggling to find common ground, consider making the conversation itself the point of common ground. "*Thanks for talking with me about this. I know it's going to be hard for you too.*" Saying that or something similar can be an effective way to create a sense of common ground.

Ask To Hear Their Side Of The Issue First.

It may seem counterintuitive for you to start a tough conversation by asking your partner to tell you how they feel about it first, but there are a couple reasons to handle the conversation this way.

First, it lets you avoid any frustration they might have about not having a chance to put their side of the story out there. If you allow them to begin the conversation with their chance to be heard, they'll not only feel better, but be more likely to let you speak your piece uninterrupted in return.

Second, hearing their side of the story before you go into your explanation of the issue will allow you to adjust what you were going to say to include points from their story. ("*You mentioned that you were especially hurt when you found out I went through your text history. I can see why you feel that way, and I think that's fair. I went through it because...*")

Adjusting your conversation this way will make your partner feel more included and heard. In turn, it will help you take the conversation in the direction you want it to go.

Resist The Urge To Argue Against Their Points.

When your partner is explaining their side of the issue, use your self-management skills to avoid correcting or arguing with them. You're going to get your chance to speak, and you letting your partner speak first was not to see if they agree to your version of the truth.

You're trying to understand where they're coming from, and why they feel the way they do. You also want them to feel heard, and you want to improve your own understanding of the issue. This not the time to prove the details of your story right, and theirs wrong.

Explain Your Side Of The Issue, So They're Able To Understand It.

When describing your side of the issue, make sure that you're doing it in a way that makes the what's, why's, and how's clear and understandable to your partner. Don't just give all the details and pain points of what you're feeling.

Do so in a way that they'll understand. Be clear, be direct, but most importantly, use your social awareness to take what you know about your partner and present details to them in a way they'll best understand. Sometimes, not much communication work is necessary, because it's easy to make your point. (*"You really hurt my feelings when I caught you texting your ex."*) Other times, you may have to more carefully and thoroughly frame your point to make it clear. (*"I know you love your mom, and I do too, but sometimes I struggle to spend long periods of time with her. I didn't grow up with a talkative mom like you did, so it's a little more difficult for me to spend time with someone who talks so much. It's nothing against her, it's just … different for me. I'm not used to answering so many questions from a parental figure, and it makes me nervous. Not because I think your mom is going to pass judgment on me for anything, although that is a small concern, but because my parents were very judgmental, so I feel this innate fearful twisting in my gut whenever a parental figure asks me questions. Does this make sense?)*

Do What You Can To Resolve The Issue, Or At Least Move It Forward.

Once you both understand each other's side of the issue, it's time to actually resolve it. If you can't resolve it now, at least move it forward. That depends on the actual issue at hand.

However, when moving toward a resolution, try to use inclusive language that continues to create common ground ("We probably shouldn't date anymore" vs. "I'm leaving you") and be sure to ask for your partner's feelings after you announce the decision you'd like to make ("We probably shouldn't date anymore. Do you feel the same way?")

Check In Afterward.

Depending on the issue you were working on, you may want to check in with your partner to see how they're feeling about the decision. If, for example, you decided to quit your full-time job to pursue freelance photography, even if your partner was okay with the decision at the time, you might want to check in again after the first cycle of bills hits, to see if they're still feeling as good when less money is coming in.

Checking in will not only show that you care, but also allow you to check if your partner has any changes in emotion since you last made the decision together. That can help alleviate any potential pent up negative emotions that could result in future emotional blowups.

3. Use Complementary Behavior To Help Ease Tense Situations With Your Partner.

By complementary behavior, we don't mean complimenting your partner with kindnesses, like telling them how attractive they are. Though they sound similar, it's actually a different word we're using: complement, meaning "to complete or fill out."

The strategy we're discussing here is how picking behavior that complements your partner's current mood can be an effective way to diffuse tense or difficult situations.

For example, your partner is in a rush to get out the door to work on time. They're panicked, and upset about being late and possibly getting in real trouble with their boss. In their hurry, they ask you for help packing up their lunch. Knowing that your partner is upset and in a rush, you choose to behave in a way that complements their mood. You spring up, quickly but calmly, and sling together a lunch for them as fast as you can. Your partner appreciates the speed and seriousness and gives you a quick kiss on the check as they hurry out the door.

What makes this behavior "complementary" and not "mirroring" is that it's not an exact match to their behavior. You have hurried to put the lunch together, but you were not in a panicked rush like your partner was at that time. Had you chosen to mirror their behavior in that way, you would have made the situation worse by adding more anxiety and chaos to an already tense situation.

Similarly, had you chosen the uncomplimentary behavior, say by telling them to relax and that it was no big deal if they had to buy lunch today, you also would have made the situation worse by invalidating their feelings and presenting yourself as an obstacle to them achieving their goals, instead of being an asset.

This is why the complementary behavior is so helpful in diffusing situations like these—it shows your partner that you understand the immediate need and vibe of the current situation, and also that you're part of their emotional support system, someone they can count on to back them up when things get tough.

4. Be Accessible (But Don't Be Afraid To Set Boundaries Too.)

It's important that your partner feel comfortable

talking about their feelings with you, both in general and specifically about your relationship. To accommodate that need, you want to make yourself accessible and open to conversation. This means responding to your partner's requests to talk with calmness, friendliness, and patience. Hear them out, even if it's not exactly what you want to be doing at the moment.

Put yourself in their shoes. They may see you there, watching TV or trying to get some extra work done on your laptop, but what they want to talk to you about is really important, and they'd really feel much better if they got it off their chest now. From that perspective, you can see how important it is that you meet their requests to talk with openness and accessibility.

That's not to say that you can't have boundaries. You're entitled to have places and/or times where you don't want to have a serious talk. Just be sure that you're consistent with those boundaries, and that those boundaries are fair to you and your partner. For example, you may have a boundary that you can't really talk on the phone at work unless it's an emergency, but you can message each other throughout the day.

5. Express Even Small Displays Of Gratitude To Make A Big Difference.

We'll end our emotional intelligence strategies with something simple, yet important—expressing even small displays of gratitude can make a big difference in your relationship. Whether it's showing that you care with small, thoughtful gifts and gestures, or it's staying on top of basic relationship courtesies like remembering to say *please* and *thank you*, these little gestures can go a long way toward building trust, affection, and goodwill with your partner.

When you're in a relationship with someone for a long time, especially when you're living with them, it can be easy to forget common formal politeness, because your relationship isn't formal and proper—it's fun and warm and comfortable and full of love. However, just because you can relax around your partner, doesn't mean that they don't enjoy hearing the word *thank you* for a favor or nice gesture. In fact, when a thank you comes from someone they love, they might even enjoy hearing it more!

This strategy might seem small, but it's very effective in building mutual respect between partners. While large, sweeping emotional gestures can have a very big positive impact on a relationship (helping a partner move, going all out for Valentine's Day, showing up when they called in sick from work and nursing them back to health), these things don't happen very often.

So, relationships depend on these small gestures of affection, respect, and kindness to set the tone and let each person know how the other feels about them. In many ways, they're an essential form of communication in relationships. So be sure to put these kinds of affectionate and polite communications out there to show your partner how you feel about them.

CHAPTER 8:

PUTTING IT ALL TOGETHER

JAMIE BRYCE

Now that we've gone over the four parts of emotional intelligence—social regulation, social awareness, self-regulation, and self-awareness—and presented strategies for improving each, let's put what you've learned together and practice solving some hypothetical relationship problems. It'll be a great way to reinforce what you've learned, as well as improve your emotional intelligence that much further.

Each of these exercises can have multiple solutions. There's no one right answer because that's not the idea here. The idea is for you to use what you've learned and see if you can use it to create a solution that you think would work best.

One last bit of advice before you jump into the exercises: Remember—the four core emotional intelligence skills are intertwined with one another. You must use all four components to come to the solutions you think will work best. So don't hesitate to go back and review the chapters if you need a refresher on any of the four key component skills.

What You'll Need For These Exercises:

Paper and a writing tool

Or

If you're reading this book on your phone, open a notetaking app, and mark your answers there. You could also use a Word document if you're reading on your laptop or desktop.

The Four Emotional Intelligence Categories And Accompanying Strategies At A Glance

Self-Awareness

Stop judging your feelings

Pay attention to your negative emotions

Don't let your current mood control you

Learn your triggers

Connect with your physical side

Self-Regulation

Diffuse negative emotions by adding time

Control how you talk to yourself

Create more emotional control by harnessing the power of positivity

Get an outside perspective from someone else

Learn to accept—and expect—change

Social Awareness

Work on your listening skills

Put yourself in your partner's shoes

Choose the right moments to make your point

Learn the rules of your partner's cultural and socioeconomic background

Get opinions on yourself from others

Social Regulation

In arguments, offer solutions

Have tough conversations

Use complementary behavior to help ease tense situations

Be accessible

Express even small displays of gratitude to make a big difference

Exercise 1: A Partner Suddenly Has To Work Late

Workaholic Wendy texts her husband, Put-Upon Preston, late on a Friday afternoon. It turns out she's got to work late, and won't be home until much later that night—maybe not until ten o'clock.

Preston is furious. Not only did Wendy promise to bring home dinner for him and their kids, but she was also supposed to watch the kids for a bit while Preston ran out to the store and picked up some groceries for the weekend. Now, Preston is left scrambling to come up with a replacement dinner for himself and the kids and is also going to have to wake up early and run out to the grocery store on a Saturday morning—one of the busiest and most annoying times to go.

And on top of that, he was also looking forward to

spending some time with his wife tonight. Now, he's not even going to see her until late, and who knows if she's going to even want to talk when she gets home. Often when Wendy works late, she comes home burnt-out, tired, and grumpy. She usually just sits on her phone for an hour, maybe watches a little TV, then goes to bed spaced out, still in a daze from working so many hours.

The worst part of all of this for Preston is that this has been happening several times a week, for months—always with short notice, and rarely with more than a quick "Sorry!" through a text. Wendy makes a lot of money at her job and is a very career-driven person.

Preston has to admit that her career success has done their marriage and family a lot of good—they've never wanted for anything and are comfortably saving money—but Preston is starting to wonder if the money is really worth it. He's really struggling to keep up with plans always changing at the last minute and with a lot of the child and home care work being dumped on his lap.

He misses his wife and how they used to be able to spend time together. They've been married for years, and Preston truly loves Wendy, but he's at a total loss for how to solve this situation, let alone tell her how he feels about her workaholism.

If you were Preston, how would you go about resolving this situation with Wendy? Take some time to write out what you'd do, starting with self-awareness action items, then progressing through the other three key emotional intelligence components.

IDEAS TO EXPLORE & INFORM YOUR ANSWERS

What self-awareness skills could Preston use to help himself understand his feelings about this situation?

- Could Preston's angry mood be getting the best of him? Is he more angry at the principle of the situation (being ignored and cast aside again) than the practical reality of the issue (ordering pizza is a completely easy and reasonable solution for a quick dinner, and it's far from the end of the world to have to go grocery shopping on a Saturday morning).

- Is the habitual cancellation of plans making this more angering than normal? Is it something that's becoming "triggering" for him? If it is becoming triggering, what are some things Preston can do to control these feelings?

- What can Preston's anger and hurt over these continuously canceled plans tell him about how feels about their relationship? And how closely aligned with reality are these feelings? Is he really doing the majority of the child and home care, or does it just feel that way sometimes, especially when plans are canceled?

How can Preston use social awareness to understand Wendy's perspective in this situation?

- How has work been going for Wendy overall? Preston knows she's been busy, but he admits he doesn't know many details past that. Would he feel better if he knew more about why she was staying so late all the time? Should he take some time to talk to her about work?

- Related to the above, how is Wendy feeling overall? She's been missing a lot of family time with working late so much. Preston knows she loves him and the kids, but Wendy tends to keep her emotions close, and doesn't really share her feelings unless Preston really digs. Could Wendy be really bothered by working late so often, or does it not bother her?

- When should Preston choose to have a hard conversation with Wendy about her constant, last-minute lateness? Right when she gets back home from working a 13-hour day in the office, or some time tomorrow when they've both had a little rest and time away from the situation?

What self-regulation skills could Preston use to help manage his feelings and behavior?

- What role is Preston's self-talk playing in making the situation worse? Currently, he's very upset, berating himself up over and over for being such a pushover, and for not having a better job himself (maybe then Wendy wouldn't have to work so hard).

- Are there any positive results here that Preston could be focusing on? He gets to spend some one-on-one bonding time with his kids, which is something he always enjoys. He's also reasonably justified to splurge on dinner— maybe he could get fancy pizza from the gourmet brick-oven place down the street. He could even order something for Wendy when she gets home.

- Should Preston accept Wendy's need to work late as a temporary truth of their marriage? While it's true that Wendy could maybe give him more notice, or at least not make definite plans if there's a chance she's going to cancel them, would Wendy really work late so much for no reason? Her career has been going great, could her schedule be a temporary birthing pain of her advancing career?

How can Preston use social regulation to try and

resolve the issues here?

- Are there any solutions or compromises Preston could offer to help ease the situation? Is there anything he could do to help Wendy spend less time in the office? Maybe he could make her lunches, so she doesn't have to spend precious time in the office looking for food? Or could he do something that would help her leave earlier in the morning so she can make it home earlier?

  And what about solutions from Wendy? Would Preston feel better about Wendy canceling if she also offered a solution, such as, "I'm going to be home late again, but I called my mother, and she's going to come over and help with the kids so you can still make it to the store"?

- Even though he doesn't really feel like it, would it be helpful in resolving the issue by thanking Wendy for working so hard for their family? After all, a 13-hour day is nothing to sneeze at.

- When it comes time to have a conversation about Wendy's habitual lateness, does Preston have a plan? Does he know what he wants to say? What common ground could he build between them both on this specific issue?

Exercise 2: Fighting Over Cleaning The Apartment

Messy Mike and Clean Calvin have been living together for a couple years. Their relationship was great when they had separate apartments, but now that they live together, Calvin is having a lot of trouble with Mike's messiness. He loves Mike, but he's not sure how much longer he can take it.

It's not just that Mike is super-messy—though he is—it's that his messiness all seems so needless and, well, lazy, to Calvin. Mike's dishes never seem to make it to the sink, let alone get rinsed off. They just pile up wherever Mike finished eating, scraps of food still on them and all. Mike always seems to be starting laundry, but never finishes it. There is always wet clothing in the washer, dry clothes in the dryer, and piles of unorganized clothes everywhere. Calvin isn't even sure which piles are clean and which piles are dirty.

The worst part for Calvin though is that Mike never wants to help clean the apartment when they have guests coming over. It always falls on Calvin to not only pick up after Mike—all his dishes and his clothes—but also to do all the rest of the cleaning in the apartment: mopping the floors, vacuuming, wiping down the kitchen, and straightening up. It's not a big apartment, but it's still a lot of work, taking Calvin several hours every week.

Calvin has tried to bring it up to Mike a couple times, but every time Mike has been very hostile, telling him to get off his back and to stop trying to control him. Their last argument about cleaning got pretty heated, and Calvin is a little nervous about bringing it up again. He knows he has to though, he just has no idea how to go about it.

If you were Calvin, how would you go about resolving this situation with Mike? Take some time to write out what you'd do, starting with self-awareness action items, then progressing through the other three key emotional intelligence components.

IDEAS TO EXPLORE & INFORM YOUR ANSWERS

What self-awareness skills could Calvin use to help himself understand his feelings about this situation?

- Whenever Calvin has to clean up after Mike, he gets so swept up in the moment (no pun intended) that he's doesn't focus much on how he's feeling. He's always in a rush to clean and prefers to focus on getting the cleaning done as fast as possible, rather than thinking about how he feels. What could Calvin do to pay better attention to his feelings?

- Calvin always feels very guilty about getting upset about having a messy house. He knows it bothers Mike when he complains about it, and he also feels it's uncool and lame to be such a neat freak. What can Calvin do to be less judgmental about his feelings?

- What can Calvin's feelings about the situation tell him about himself and his relationship with Mike? Why is he dreading having a simple conversation about cleaning? What does that say about him, and what could he do to change for the better?

How can Calvin use social awareness to understand Mike's perspective in this situation?

- Why is Mike so messy? Has he been like this his whole life? Calvin thinks about what he knows about Mike's childhood and doesn't think he could have been as messy then. Mike's mother has a very strong personality, and based on what Calvin has seen of her and Mike's relationship, they would have fought constantly and aggressively about every little piece of trash.

- When they've fought previously about cleaning, Mike has said "get off my back" and "stop trying to control me." Those are pretty self-explanatory statements, but they're also pretty aggressive and dramatic considering it's just a conversation about cleaning up dishes and laundry. What could be making Mike react that way? Is he an inherently dramatic person, or could Calvin be pushing Mike's buttons in other ways that are making him react that way?

- Sometimes Calvin wonders if Mike really is that messy, or if it's him that is a clean freak. They are in their early 20s after all—most men their age aren't known for their cleanliness. Is there a way Calvin could get an answer to this question?

What self-regulation skills could Calvin use to help manage his feelings and behavior?

- What role is Calvin's passive aggressive self-talk playing in making the situation worse? Whenever he's cleaning, Calvin quite literally talks to himself, saying things out loud like, "Oh, I guess I'll just do it all! I'll clean the whole place because I'm your personal maid. That's me, Cleaning Calvin, the live-in maid." Whether Mike hears Calvin when he talks to himself like this or not, he doesn't react. He just stares at the TV, his jaw tightly set.

- Are there any positive results here that Calvin could be focusing on? Certainly having to clean up after your partner is terrible, but is Mike doing anything positive that Calvin could focus on? Is he doing the cooking? Paying more than his share of the bills? Is he wonderful to spend time with when they're not fighting about cleaning?

- Calvin knows this one-sided cleaning situation is not sustainable. Eventually, it may come down to this cleaning problem getting solved, or Calvin walking out. Calvin absolutely does not want to break up, which means the cleaning situation has to get solved. What can he do to prepare for that emotionally?

How can Calvin use social regulation to try and resolve the issues here?

- When arguing about cleaning, are there solutions Calvin could offer Mike that could help ease the tension? Is there anything Calvin could do to make cleaning easier for Mike? Are there other chores that Calvin could suggest that Mike do instead of cleaning?

- Because their last few fights on the subject have been so bad, Calvin has shut himself off from talking about it. After calming down himself, Mike has approached Calvin a few times to talk about things, but before anything happens, Calvin makes an excuse, like having to run off for a time-sensitive errand. What could Calvin do differently here?

- How can Calvin plan for this hard conversation? What can he do to create common ground between them? How can he make sure that Mike feels heard?

Exercise 3: Asking To Be Exclusive, Or "Officially" Becoming A Couple

Singular Sasha and Free-Rolling Fred have been seeing each other for a couple months, maybe going on 15 or so dates over the course of that time. Things are going great.

They're having fun, really clicking and getting along well. There's only one problem: when they started dating, neither was looking for anything serious, but now, Sasha wants to take the next step and become an official couple.

When Sasha and Fred started dating, they were both

committed to being single, not interested in having a serious relationship of any kind. Both of them were seeing other people. Both knew that and were okay with that arrangement, at least at the beginning. Now though, Sasha thinks she's developing more serious feelings for Fred, and she wants more than their current casual arrangement.

She wants to spend more time with Fred. She wants him to meet her friends and family. And most of all, she doesn't want to share him with other women anymore. Her problem is, she's not sure if Fred is on the same page.

Fred and Sasha haven't had many serious conversations, but from the few serious talks they have had, Sasha feels like Fred is not interested in settling down. He's said that he recently got out of a long-term relationship about a year ago, and he'd been with that person for almost ten years. The breakup was painful and took a long time to resolve and heal. Fred has said that for now, he's really not interested in anything serious. He's just not ready.

Only Sasha thinks he seems ready. He's getting more affectionate the more they see each other and is suggesting activities that are less like "dates' and more like "couples activities" like going with him to the farmer's market on Sunday morning or meeting up at the gym to work out together a bit before going to work. He's bringing her small silly gifts, like little sentimental pieces of memorabilia from their earlier dates, and they're starting to text back and forth during the day just for fun.

Sasha is feeling very confused and has no idea what to do. On the one hand, she feels like Fred was very clear about his desire to not have a serious relationship. She doesn't want to say that's not good enough for her and risk losing what they currently have together.

But on the other hand, he said that very early on when they were dating, so maybe he doesn't mean it anymore? Also, he certainly isn't acting like he only wants something casual. Some days, Sasha feels like they're already an actual couple.

Sasha knows she has to address this with Fred soon. Her feelings for him are only getting stronger. But, she's very afraid of risking the relationship by putting herself out there and making it clear that she wants more than Fred may be willing to offer.

If you were Sasha, how would you go about resolving this situation with Fred? Take some time to write out what you'd do, starting with self-awareness action items, then progressing through the other three key emotional intelligence components.

IDEAS TO EXPLORE & INFORM YOUR ANSWERS

What self-awareness skills could Sasha use to help herself understand her feelings about this situation?

- This problem with Fred is making Sasha crazy. She's losing sleep over her fear of losing him and is starting to feel guilty every time she sees him because she feels like she's lying to him— pretending to feel one way, while actually feeling another. What could she do to help acknowledge these feelings, without torturing herself with them?

- Thinking about the mixed signals that Fred has been sending her, Sasha is wondering if *she* has been sending mixed signals to *him*. Since she's realized her feelings for Fred, how has she been acting? Has she been too standoffish for fear of losing him? Or too affectionate, which risks revealing her true feelings? What is the best way for her to act?

- What can Sasha learn about herself from her fear of losing Fred? Is this fear just about losing Fred, or does she have trouble speaking her mind in other tough situations? If it's the latter, what does that mean for Sasha? What could she do to become more comfortable with speaking her mind?

How can Sasha use social awareness to understand Fred's recent behavior and figure out if he's interested in a more serious relationship or not?

- Sasha isn't sure if she's reading too much into Fred's recent romantic gestures or not. What are some ways she could analyze Fred's behavior to really pin down and define his mood and feelings in a given moment?

  For example, when they go to the Farmer's market next Sunday morning, what should Sasha look for in Fred to see if he's interested in dating her more seriously? Could she put herself in his shoes, and think about what he would do if he were trying to convince her to date him more seriously?

- What's a good time for Sasha to pick to have this conversation with Fred? Should she just blurt it out on one of their next dates, or should she try and pick an optimal time and location to have the conversation? If it's the latter, what times and places would be good, and why?

- Sasha has kept her problems with Fred to herself. She's starting to feel very alone and trapped in her own head. What could she do to alleviate these feelings? And in the future, what could she do to realize she's feeling trapped in her head in the first place? Are these feelings affecting her behavior around Fred or the way he receives her lately?

What self-regulation skills could Sasha use to help manage her feelings and behavior?

- Sasha is very tied up in thinking about the worst-case scenario of her and Fred breaking up. What are some positives that she could focus on instead? What would it mean if Fred is interested in a more serious relationship, but is also afraid to bring it up?

- Every time Sasha sees Fred, she gets swept up in her emotions and is completely hijacked by her strong affection for him. How can Sasha create some distance from her emotions and actually come to a rational decision about what she wants to say to Fred?

- Can Sasha emotionally prepare for the worst-case scenario, which is Fred and her breaking up because he doesn't want a more serious relationship? What would the breakup mean for Sasha?

How can Sasha use social regulation to try and resolve the issue with Fred?

- How can Sasha adjust the signals she's sending Fred to make sure that 1) It seems like she's open and receptive to his increased affection and 2) She seems open to serious conversation about their relationship status?

- How can Sasha plan for the conversation about their relationship status with Fred? Since they talked a little bit about their relationship goals and desires when they first started dating, could a follow up on that conversation be a good starting point? Or, would you approach the conversation differently?

- Is Sasha giving Fred the right feedback for all the small affectionate gestures he's paying her? What could she do to make sure that she's showing appropriate gratitude? What value would showing that gratitude have?

Exercise 4: What Happens When Mom-In-Law Keeps Asking For Money?

Cashed-Out Carrie and Loyal Laura have a problem: Laura's mom keeps asking the couple for money, and it's really starting to bother Carrie. The couple has been married for a few years, and they've been living together for even longer. They combined their finances years ago, which had been working out great until the problem with Laura's mom popped up.

Laura's mom always seems to need money. Sixty dollars here. Two-fifty there. Once or twice, she asked for $1,500. It has been going on for years, and it's really starting to add up and affect the couple's finances. Laura doesn't seem to mind—she's just glad she's able to help her mom, but Carrie is not sure how much longer she can take it.

Carrie knows that she should feel more sympathy for Laura's mom. She's an older woman who's been single for a long time, and through a mix of poor health and bad luck, has had trouble holding down a career. She was very good to Laura as a child, making sure she had the best childhood possible.

But now, it feels like their roles have flipped and Laura is spending all her time and resources caring for her mother. Laura's mother is only 63, which Carrie feels is young enough that she should be able to take care of herself but that's not the real issue.

What upsets Carrie the most is that Laura's mother always says she'll pay back the money, but never does. She just takes more and more money, with barely a thank you, as if she's entitled to it because she's Laura's mother.

Carrie has brought up her feelings about this situation with Laura's mom a few times, and it has not gone well. Laura is very protective and defensive about her mother and doesn't see any other option besides giving her the money she needs. While Carrie isn't suggesting that Laura cut her mother off, she also doesn't see how these constant micro-loans can possibly be necessary unless Laura's financial skills are just ridiculously stupid. She's a grown woman, there's no reason she should need to "borrow" $60 every two weeks. The argument usually escalates from there, ending in a big fight with one of them sleeping on the couch.

Carrie is at a loss for what to do. She knows she has to figure out how to fix this problem in their relationship with some kind of compromise, but she has no idea how to come up with one that will make them both happy. She doesn't even know how to start the conversation. Every time she's tried, it's ended in a big fight that just made everything worse.

If you were Carrie, how would you go about resolving this situation with Laura and her mother? Take some time to write out what you'd do, starting with self-awareness action items, then progressing through the other three key emotional intelligence components.

IDEAS TO EXPLORE & INFORM YOUR ANSWERS

What self-awareness skills could Carrie use to help herself understand her feelings about this situation?

- Every time Carrie thinks about this lending situation with Laura and her mom, she becomes completely overwhelmed with anger. She loses all ability to think about anything else, and finds herself seething for hours. What are some strategies Carrie can use to acknowledge her anger, without becoming overwhelmed by it?

- How can Carrie use this problem with Laura and her mom to learn more about herself and her own emotions? Is she just upset about the money that's being lost, or could she have other issues?

  Could part of her anger be about Laura being very tight with money when it's Carrie who wants to spend it, but then Laura doesn't have a problem lending her mother money, no questions asked. If that's the case, what should Carrie do about those feelings?

- Carrie is starting to notice other things related to Laura's mom or money that are starting to set her off. She dislikes looking at her bank account because it always reminds her of the money they're losing. She has trouble going to family events with her in-laws because it's getting very hard to be around her mother-in-law. Is there anything Carrie can do about these triggering events, or are they just a sign of how badly Carrie needs to resolve this problem?

How can Carrie use social awareness to understand Laura's perspective on the situation?

- Carrie was never as close to her mother as Laura is with hers. But, she knows it's not uncommon. She's thinking about asking her friend Ben about his relationship with his parents. She's known Ben for a long time and knows that he's very close to his mother.

What are some questions Carrie could ask Ben about his relationship with his mother that could be helpful in understanding Laura's relationship with her mother? Could she ask for other advice too, like how she could cope with such a difficult in-law situation?

- How does this argument look from Laura's perspective? How would it make her feel that giving a little extra money to her mother every month frustrates her partner of many years? What about the point that the conversations about loaning money always turn into a yelling match, with Laura feeling like she's not being heard.

- Laura was solely raised by her mother for almost her entire life, of which Carrie is aware. They had very little money, but Laura's mom made sure that what money they did have was spent on Laura. Carrie knows these financial hardships made mother and daughter very close, and she sees that Laura's mom has made tremendous sacrifices for her daughter in the past with no hesitation. What else could this fact tell Carrie about her partner's emotions toward her mother?

What self-regulation skills could Carrie use to help manage her feelings and behavior?

- Carrie is legitimately worried that they're going to start missing bill payments because of the money they're giving Laura's mom, apart from all the sleep she's losing over it. What are some strategies Carrie can use to make herself feel better about her financial stress or to help herself sleep better?

- Instead of letting her anger bubble up, is there anything positive about this situation that Carrie could focus on? How does it make her feel that Laura is so loving and loyal to her mother?

- When Carrie is feeling hijacked by her emotions of anger, what are some strategies she can use to help break free? How can she use the time to separate herself from the overwhelming feelings of anger so she can have the opportunity to think of solutions to their argument?

How can Carrie use social regulation to try and resolve this issue with Laura?

- Are there any compromises or solutions that Carrie could propose that could help take some of the tension and anger out of the argument?

Or, what are some reasonable concessions she should expect Laura to make that could ease their disagreement?

- Every time Carrie and Laura talk about the problem, it quickly leads to a fight. What can Carrie do to keep the conversation from escalating into a fight the next time? And if a fight does happen—what can Carrie do to diffuse the situation?

- When it comes time to have this conversation, how much practical information should Carrie prepare? Is it important for her to know the exact amount of money that they've lent Laura's mother, or will that information only make the conversation worse? How can she create a sense of common ground between herself and Laura?

CONCLUSION

JAMIE BRYCE

Great job. You have now made it through to the end of *Couples Guide To Emotional Intelligence*. Let's hope it was informative and able to provide you with all of the tools you need to achieve your goals of making your relationships more enjoyable, more stable, and longer lasting.

Keep in mind all the lessons you've learned from this book. You've learned the scientific history of emotional intelligence, gaining an appreciation for its place and importance in psychological discourse and study. You learned just what emotional intelligence is, and why it's a critical skill needed for improving your relationship. Lastly, you studied the four core components of emotional intelligence and learned strategies on how to apply them in your life. Then, everything was concluded with some exercises at the end of the book, letting you put everything you learned into practice.

The next step is to put the strategies, tips, and habits you've learned in this book into practice yourself in your current relationship! So get out there and impress your partner with your new-found sense of self-awareness, wow them with your improved ability to regulate your emotions, dazzle them with your deeper empathy and understanding of their feelings, and make them fall in love with you all over again with your increased skill in cooperating, understanding, and managing your relationship!

If you found this book useful in any way, please leave a review on Amazon letting us know how much you loved it!

Be on the lookout for more books by Jamie Bryce on Amazon and Audible.

.

Made in United States
North Haven, CT
21 December 2021